Thematic Activities for Student Portfolios

by Kathy Balsamo

Pieces of
Learning

1996 Revised Edition
© 1994 Pieces of Learning
Cover Design Pat Bleidorn & Stan Balsamo
ISBN 1-880505-11-8
All rights reserved. Printed in the USA.
Printing No. 5432
Pieces of Learning is a Division of
Creative Learning Consultants Inc.
1-800-729-5137

Thematic Activities for Student Portfolios
Table of Contents

How to Use this Book NOW	**6**	Graphic Organizer for Curriculum Development	22
Educators' Jargon	8	Global Topics - Global Activities & Products	24
Learning Styles	10	Resources	26
Taxonomy Verbs & Activities	14	Thematic Units	27
Web of Activities	16	Learner Outcomes	28
Web of Products	17	Unit Guidelines	29
The Language of Questioning	18	Thematic Webbing	30
Question Web	20	Portfolios	33
Government Question Web	21	Assessment Criteria	36

Thematic Activity Webs

Getting a Good Start	45	Theater	75	*The Lorax*	100
Animals	47	Trails from the Past	77	*The Great Kapok Tree*	101
Backyard Beasties	49	Washington D.C.	79	*Tree of Life - The World*	
Bodyworks	51	Water	81	*of The African Baobab*	102
Dinosaurs	53	Weather	83	*Desert Giant - The World*	
Famous People	55	The Circus	85	*of the Saguaro Cactus*	103
Flowers	57	We are Multi-cultural	87	End of Year Web	104
Food for Thought	59	Rocks and Minerals	89	**Appendix**	
Jazz-Jazz-Jazz	61	Contemporary Social		Activity Cards	105
Government	63	Studies	91	Journal Entries	106
Literature Awareness	65	Thingamajigs . . .	93	Verbal/Linguistic	107
Fun With Math	67	The Tropical Rain Forest	95	Bodily/Kinesthetic	
Matter & Energy	69	Remembering	97	Visual/Spatial	108
The Orient Connection	71	Where in the World?	98	Logical/Mathematical	
Plants and Trees	73	Ways to Do Book Reports	99	Intrapersonal	109
				Musical/Rhythmic	
				Interpersonal	110

Reminiscing . . .

From the 70's to the present . . .

We've come a long way, lady.

A special dedication . . .

and thank you . . .

to my partner and soul mate

Nancy Johnson

My personal spirit lifter . . .

This one's for you!

What next? *Tupperware?*

Thinking . . .

As a teacher of math, I could never understand why we were to take DAILY math grades; enter them in a grade book over a 6-week period over one or maybe two concepts (like addition and subtraction); then average those 30 grades and label a student a "B" math student!

Why did we grade/evaluate/assess the LEARNING? Why didn't we just see if and how the daily work was done, and in a final test EVALUATE the SKILL—addition? Then Joe could be an "A" addition student; a "C" subtraction student; and a "B" multi-step word problem student. That would translate possibly into a "B" math student! But he would also know which of the math skills were strengths and which were weaknesses when he went on to multiplication and division. And why didn't teachers—not textbooks—create multi-step word problems that dealt with other subject matter or at least REALITY in Bartonville, Illinois or Baytown, Texas?

After 25 years, PORTFOLIOS and THEMATIC UNITS have come on the academic scene to address my questions about the difference between assessing and evaluating skills, processes, and products; and I hope they're here to stay. I think GREAT teachers have always used both; they just didn't have the 90s label for them.

But now we do. Hang on to them! Give them a chance! Get students and parents involved in them! Let them know you are using them, why you are using them, and how they work. Show them the differences between ASSESSMENT and EVALUATION and why you use both. And get both students and parents involved in criteria development, product selection, and product assessment.

and Thanking . . .

. . . **Shirley Bendau**, Major Contributor of the "webs" you see in this book

. . . my husband **Stan Balsamo** for his unending patience with me, my computer knowledge (just enough to keep me in constant trouble) and the millions of bytes that make up this book on my hard drive!

. . . my parents **Cliff and Louise Jackson** for their unconditional support and amazement

— Kathy Balsamo

How to Use This Book NOW

Use the **Learning Styles** *p. 10*
• to **assess** student styles and **identify** preferred activities, thinking processes, products
• to **enrich** learning by presenting activities that require use of new styles

Use the **Questioning Techniques** *p. 18*
• to allow students to begin to think at a higher, ACTIVE level
• to increase the kinds of questions you ask in the classroom and students ask themselves, each other, and you

Use the **Graphic Organizer for Curriculum Development** *p. 22*
• to complete the question/activity/product process for all themes you use
• to assign different activities or parts of activities to cooperative learning group members. Match **learning styles** with **activities** and **products** to complement student abilities

Use the **Learner Outcomes** and **Unit Objectives** *p. 28*
• to design relevant, active learning
• to be accountable to administration, parents, community, and students for what goes on in your classroom

Use the **Assessment Criteria** *p. 36*
• as a framework and then add your own tangible standards
• to help to explain to and interpret for parents, evaluation standards that complement the expectations and values of your school and community
• to provide accountable, tangible standards against which all types of products can be measured

The **Portfolio** Activity *p. 42*
• Have students choose the thematic activity they would like to pursue or have the student pose a new question, activity, and product. Copy the activity onto the activity page.
• Indicate the objective the activity meets.
• Decide what learning style(s) the activity best uses.
• List the product(s) the student has chosen.
• Prior to the activity agree on assessment criteria for the process and product.
• After the product has been completed, have the student and teacher complete an assessment. Use any other assessment criteria you or the student chooses. Put the Portfolio Activity Page and the work, picture of the work, or description of the work in the Portfolio.

Use the **Icons** to discover examples of subject area activities *p. 46-94*

The *microscope* icon indicates a science activity.

The *book* icon indicates a language arts activity.

The *people* indicate a social studies activity.

The *palette* indicates a visual arts activity.

The *masks* and *treble clef* indicate a performing arts activity.

The *dollar sign, clock, numbers, graph,* and *ruler* indicate a math activity.

Reproduce the **Thematic Activity Webs** *p. 46-104*
- as is for individuals or groups to supplement your existing unit
- as a transparency for the total group
- on colored paper
- enlarged for a bulletin board
- add to or replace activities with "More Questions"
- as a mobile for open house
- laminated on file folders for a learning center
- as "removable" activities — use "Spray Mount" on the back of the paper; cut out the activity shapes; "attach" them to the wall, blackboard, or bulletin board; have students choose activities by taking them from the web (to do as independent study, partner activities, or cooperative learning group work)

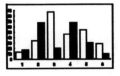

Educators' Jargon

abstract random learner - learning through feelings and imagination and others (Gregorc p. 10)

abstract sequential learner - learning through thoughts and symbols; logical; holistic; intellectual learner (Gregorc p. 10)

acceleration - covering the curriculum at a fast pace eliminating replication and excess drill

active learning - allowing students to participate in the planning, learning, and assessment process

assessment vs evaluation - assessment is a process—it includes testing measures such as tests and surveys, observation such as log entries, and samples of student performance; evaluation is a judging of all that has been gathered in the assessment process; it is analogous to an end product

authentic assessment - evaluating or assessing product/outcome that is a learning activity that calls for thinking above the knowledge level and is worthy of doing

brainstorming - activity that stimulates creative and high level thinking; generation of ideas with no right or wrong judgment attached to the ideas

collaboration - groups working together—students and teacher, students and students, adults and students—in a less structured environment than cooperative learning groups

compacting - covering the same amount of materials or activities in less time

concrete random learner - independent; leader; original thinker; experimental (Gregorc p. 10)

concrete sequential learner - down-to-earth, practical learner; conventional, conservative, perfectionist (Gregorc p. 10)

convergent thinking - coming to one particular answer by eliminating ideas

cooperative learning - heterogeneous learning groups, usually of four, in which students take responsibility for achieving shared group goals

creative problem solving - the process of applying previously acquired knowledge to new and unfamiliar situations

creative thinking - thinking fluently, flexibly, taking risks, being able to detail, and being original; uses divergent and convergent thinking

critical thinking - evaluation & consideration of data; 5 steps recognize the problem, formulate hypotheses, gather data, test & evaluate, draw conclusions; requires creative thinking

differentiate - moving beyond factual information; accelerating, applying learned knowledge, telescoping, postholing

divergent - coming to many answers by adding to ideas

graphic organizer - non-linear way of organizing; a visual design of verbal statements to organize (flow chart, mindmap, cluster, web, continuum)

inclusion - including all students in the same curriculum and providing for all their needs

integrating curriculum - linking one content area into another content area

kinesthetic learning - using the body in the learning process

learner outcome - instructional objective; intended learning; what is expected as a result of instruction; measurable cognitive and affective objectives

life long learning - life support skills - skills needed for the 21st century: flexible thinking; self esteem, planning, dealing with change, persistence, risk taking

multiple intelligences - Dr. Howard Gardner's theory explores multiple intelligences: visual/spatial; musical/rhythmic; interpersonal; bodily/kinesthetic; intrapersonal; verbal/linguistic; and mathematical/logical

portfolio - authentic assessment of what a student can do over a period of time; informal and formal collection of products for assessment and documentation of achievement

postholing - in depth investigation of subjects, ideas, or problems

process - learning how to learn through a systematic development of specific thinking skills

product - the final outcome of an assignment

Taxonomy of Educational Objectives - a means of classifying educational goals *(see pages 14-15)* in the Cognitive Domain including knowledge, comprehension, application, analysis, synthesis, and evaluation and the Affective Domain including receiving, responding, valuing, organizing, and characterizing; developed by Dr. Benjamin Bloom and his associates Engelhart, Furst, Hill and Krathwohl

technological learner - learning by using tools that include tape recorders, video recorders, computers, long-distance satellites, FAX machines, projectors, and other technology

thematic unit - using a content topic or concept as a theme and infusing that topic into other content areas; lessons are planned around the theme and then across the content area allowing for postholing (in depth study) and telescoping (accelerated study)

Three Rs for the 21st century - Ability to find, use, analyze and present information
- Ability to form meaningful and working relationships with each other
- Ability to communicate effectively with others

verbal learner - learning by listening, writing, and speaking

visual learner - imaging ideas and concepts graphically in our minds

web (cluster, mindmap) - graphic orgainzer of ideas branching out and piggybacking

Add New Terms Here

Learning Styles

Use the next pages with students. They will become aware of characteristics, activities, and products associated with particular learning styles. Then they may be better able to choose activities and products best suited for their learning style and for assessment in portfolios. They can also choose activities and products from **other** learning styles. Those products may be included in portfolios as affective examples of flexibility, risk taking, and changes in attitude toward learning. Have students circle verbs, activities, products, and descriptors that best describe them. Then list them on the Student Inventory page and place the list in their portfolios.   **Adapted from the work of Dr. Anthony Gregorc*

1 — **Concrete random** learners generally like. . .

to complete some kind of product for their classes

to be creative

to brainstorm ideas

to take risks

to do things by trial and error

to solve problems alone

to stay away from achievement and IQ tests.

2 — **Abstract random** learners generally like. . .

to listen to, learn from, and respond to their classmates

to work in a group

to read short reading assignments

to use emotions and intuition

to have lots of things going on at once.

3 — **Abstract sequential** learners generally like. . .

to read lots of different kinds of books

to listen to audio tapes

to listen to lectures

to see slides

to see filmstrips

to help other students understand what they have read

to find "the" answer to a problem

to look at things logically.

4 — **Concrete Sequential** learners generally like. . .

to follow step by step directions

to take notes

to draw charts

to make outlines

to participate in "hands on" experiences

to know the grading system, have organized teachers.

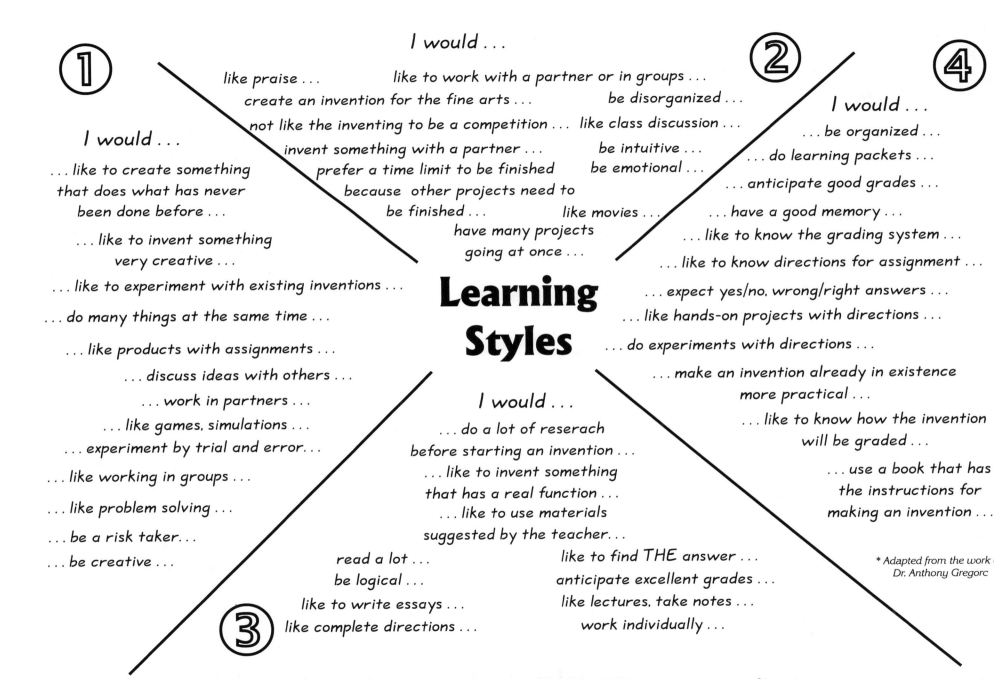

Learning Styles

①

I would . . .

. . . like to create something that does what has never been done before . . .

. . . like to invent something very creative . . .

. . . like to experiment with existing inventions . . .

. . . do many things at the same time . . .

. . . like products with assignments . . .

. . . discuss ideas with others . . .

. . . work in partners . . .

. . . like games, simulations . . .

. . . experiment by trial and error . . .

. . . like working in groups . . .

. . . like problem solving . . .

. . . be a risk taker . . .

. . . be creative . . .

I would . . .

like praise . . .

create an invention for the fine arts . . .

not like the inventing to be a competition . . .

invent something with a partner . . .

prefer a time limit to be finished because other projects need to be finished . . .

like to work with a partner or in groups . . .

be disorganized . . .

like class discussion . . .

be intuitive . . .

be emotional . . .

like movies . . .

have many projects going at once . . .

②

④

I would . . .

. . . be organized . . .

. . . do learning packets . . .

. . . anticipate good grades . . .

. . . have a good memory . . .

. . . like to know the grading system . . .

. . . like to know directions for assignment . . .

. . . expect yes/no, wrong/right answers . . .

. . . like hands-on projects with directions . . .

. . . do experiments with directions . . .

. . . make an invention already in existence more practical . . .

. . . like to know how the invention will be graded . . .

. . . use a book that has the instructions for making an invention . . .

* Adapted from the work of Dr. Anthony Gregorc

③

I would . . .

. . . do a lot of reserach before starting an invention . . .

. . . like to invent something that has a real function . . .

. . . like to use materials suggested by the teacher . . .

read a lot . . .

be logical . . .

like to write essays . . .

like complete directions . . .

like to find THE answer . . .

anticipate excellent grades . . .

like lectures, take notes . . .

work individually . . .

Which descriptors best describe YOU? Circle ideas you like best.

11

Which Learning Style Products . . .

Verbal

interview
oral report
perform
write stories, essays, lists
speech
Readers' Theater

Hands-on

scrapbook
information cube
game
papier mache
model
puppet
demonstration

Technological

satellite learning
FAX machines
computers
video recorders
tape recorders
overhead projectors
science equipment

Visual

pantomime	mobile
chart	picture
video	collage
diorama	cartoon
poster	map

. . . do you like to do best?

Circle ideas you like best.

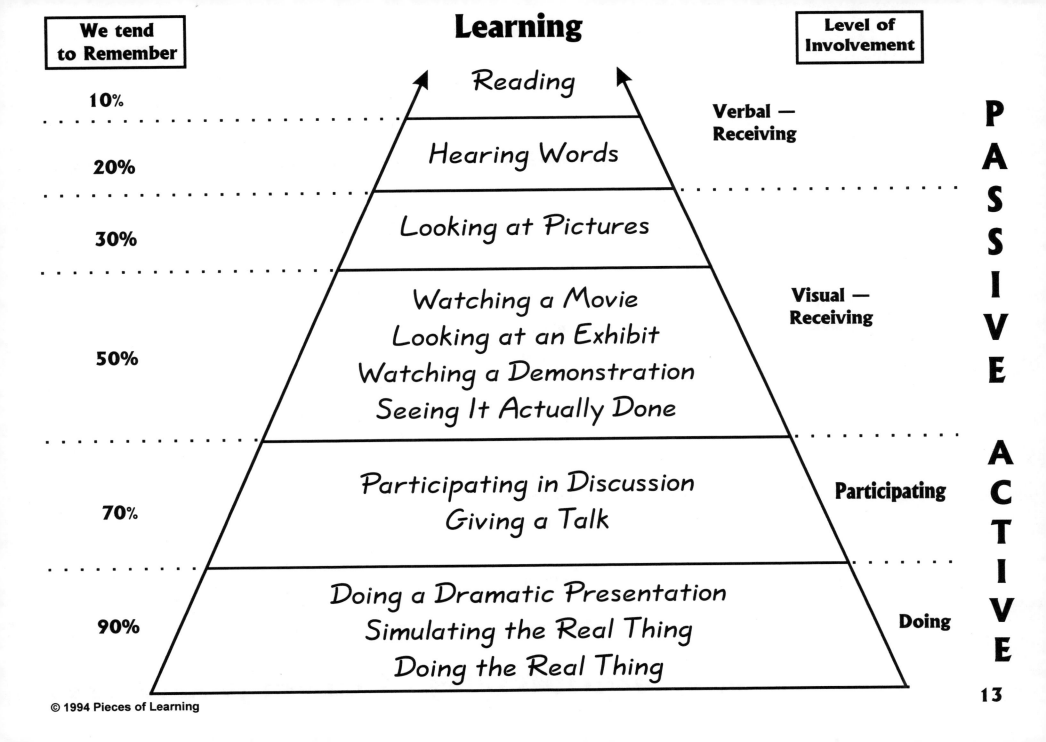

Learning

13

Taxonomy of Learning - Representative Verbs

Knowledge	Comprehension	Application	Analysis	Synthesis	Evaluation
fill in	change	apply	analyze	compose	assess
find	conclude	arrange	discover	construct	award
group	describe	choose	distinguish	create	choose
identify	explain	classify	examine	develop	decide
label	extend	construct	identify	devise	evaluate
list	group	employ	infer	hypothesize	grade
locate	outline	experiment	inspect	make	rank
match	reorganize	make use of	reduce	originate	rate
name	restate	solve	relate	produce	put (in
recite	reword	try	separate		order)
say	summarize	use			
tell					
write					

Circle verbs that best describe what you like to do. List them on your Student Inventory page.

Taxonomy of Learning - Representative Activities

Knowledge

question/answer discussions

working in workbooks or on
  worksheets

playing games and working
  puzzles

practicing through drill

reading

Comprehension

debating ideas

creative drama

working in small groups

estimating, predicting

paraphrasing selections

Application

simulations

experimenting

building models

interviewing

classifying

role playing

Analysis

identifying problems

outlining

deducing

compare/contrast

Synthesis

creating original plans

identifying goals

showing changes

combining

Evaluation

brainstorming criteria

using criteria
  (to evaluate self and peer projects)

Circle activities you best like to do. List them on your Student Inventory page.

Activities

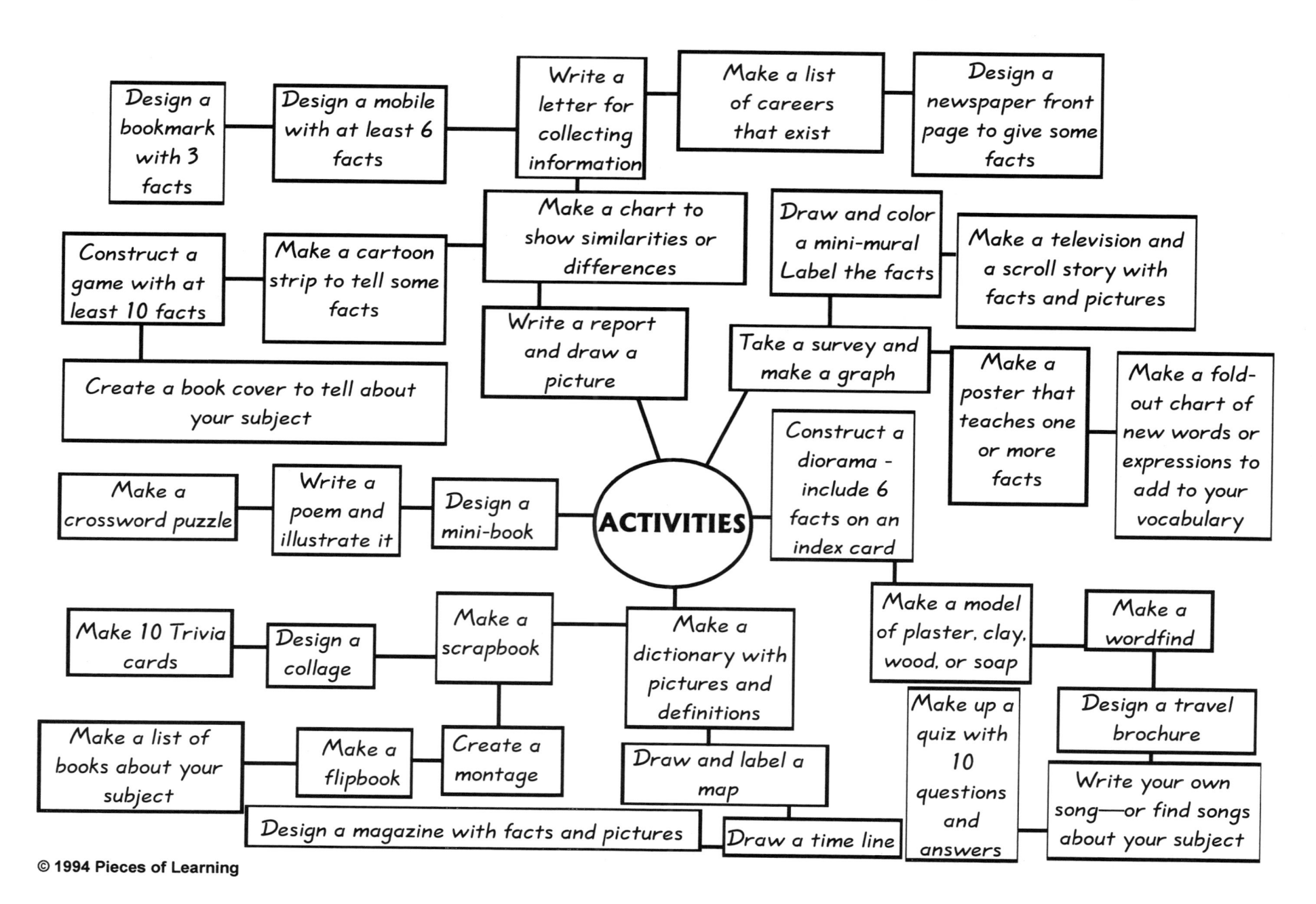

Design a bookmark with 3 facts

Design a mobile with at least 6 facts

Write a letter for collecting information

Make a list of careers that exist

Design a newspaper front page to give some facts

Make a chart to show similarities or differences

Draw and color a mini-mural Label the facts

Make a television and a scroll story with facts and pictures

Construct a game with at least 10 facts

Make a cartoon strip to tell some facts

Write a report and draw a picture

Take a survey and make a graph

Make a poster that teaches one or more facts

Make a fold-out chart of new words or expressions to add to your vocabulary

Create a book cover to tell about your subject

Make a crossword puzzle

Write a poem and illustrate it

Design a mini-book

ACTIVITIES

Construct a diorama - include 6 facts on an index card

Make 10 Trivia cards

Design a collage

Make a scrapbook

Make a dictionary with pictures and definitions

Make a model of plaster, clay, wood, or soap

Make a wordfind

Make a list of books about your subject

Make a flipbook

Create a montage

Draw and label a map

Make up a quiz with 10 questions and answers

Design a travel brochure

Write your own song—or find songs about your subject

Design a magazine with facts and pictures

Draw a time line

© 1994 Pieces of Learning

Color in blue products you like to produce. Color in green 6 products you would like to try. Include these on your Student Inventory.

Products

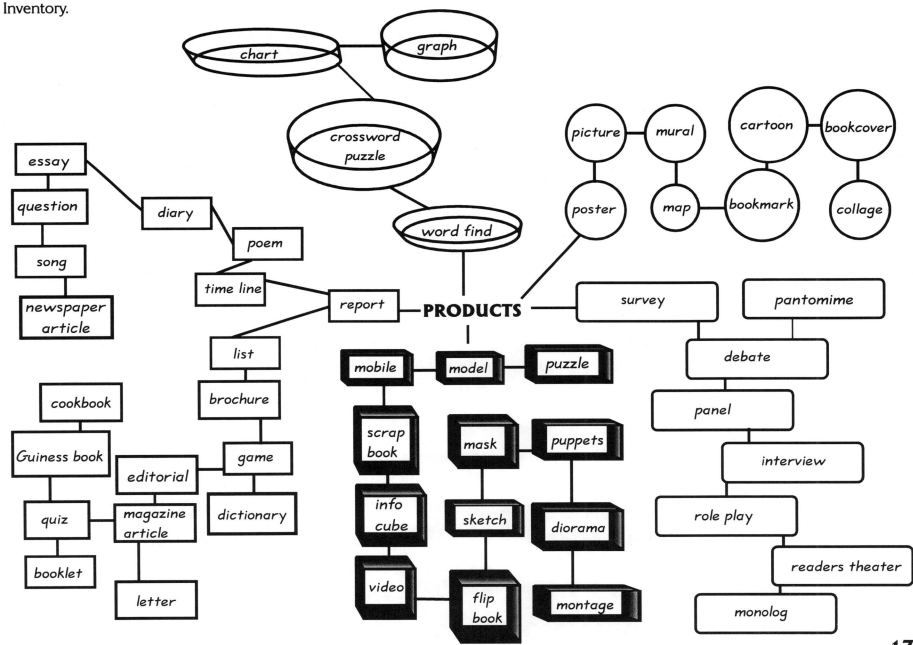

chart — graph

crossword puzzle

word find

essay — question — song — newspaper article

diary — poem

time line — report — **PRODUCTS**

picture — mural
poster
cartoon — bookcover
map — bookmark
collage

survey

pantomime

debate

panel

interview

role play

readers theater

monolog

list

brochure

game

dictionary

cookbook

Guiness book

editorial

magazine article

quiz

booklet

letter

mobile — model — puzzle

scrap book

info cube

video

mask — puppets

sketch

flip book

diorama

montage

The Language of Questioning

The divergent questioning process is most effective when teachers start teaching for questions instead of answers. The process includes:

Quality Questions   Compare/Contrast Questions

Feelings/Opinions/Personification Questions   What Would Happen If Questions

Quantity questions serve as a readiness for the others. The key to this particular kind of questioning is **Brainstorming**. Proficiency in brainstorming lays the foundation for all other types of divergent questioning. All four kinds of differentiated questions attempt to change questioning from a Passive to **Active** mode. Passive questions are those the teacher asks. Students ask active questions.

I. Quantity Questions

Quantity questions are basically **Listing** questions. However, most teachers ask only Reproductive quantity questions. Teachers ask students to reproduce some knowledge or information they already know or should know. Consequently, those kinds of questions slight high level thinking and creativity.

   Example — List the parts of a clock.

The other kind of quantity questions is **Productive**. The students **Brainstorm** as many different ideas as possible—no right/no wrong answers. Teachers should ask both kinds of quantity questions, balancing reproductive and productive thinking.

   *Example — **What are all the ways to tell time other than looking at a clock?***

The questioning process becomes ACTIVE when students create their own lists of quantity questions. The teacher provides the answers (ideas) and the students supply the questions. In this case, the focus is on the questions, not the responses.

   *Example — **Make a list of questions a grandfather clock might ask a digital clock.***

II. Compare/Contrast Questions

Compare/contrast questions (how two things are alike and how they are different) are ideal examples of the development of a simple process into a complex one. They move from the Concrete to the Abstract. The following examples compare/contrast two objects, ideas, or concepts from the same category. Gradually progress to more difficult/complex categories that require **Forced Associations.**

   Example — Ask students to choose partners. Have them hold out and examine their left hands.
   Ask partners to compare/ contrast hands. Share responses with their partners.

Compare/contrast their hands to cooking tongs. Ask students to compare/contrast cooking tongs and a can opener.
Forced Association — *How are computers and can openers alike/different?*

III. Feelings/Opinions/Personification Questions

Feelings/opinion/personification questions are a powerful, exciting teacher tool. They are fun and challenging for teachers to model as well as teach. Researchers characterize these as VIEWPOINT or PERSONAL INVOLVEMENT questions. They literally pull teacher and student together on an emotional level.

Example (Feelings)   *Which season of the year makes you feel happy? Which makes you feel tired? Which makes you feel lazy? WHY?*

Example (Opinion)   *In your opinion, should state government pass a law forcing bicycle riders to wear helmets?*

Example (Personification)   *How would a flagpole feel about a 1000 pound flag?*

There is an interesting "fringe benefit" with these questions. Feelings/opinions/personification questions will open the door to **Motivation**. The hidden force that motivates is **Emotion**. These questions are charged with emotion, especially when they fit the student's age, interests, and abilities.

IV. What Would Happen If...? Questions

Kids will say these questions are just plain fun. To completely let go of rigid thinking patterns, to break traditional mind sets, to open the mind to an "anything goes" attitude has to be one of life's greatest highs. The teacher who facilitates "what would happen if?" questions must accept the responsibility as leader and model for laughter and creative thinking and questioning.

Example — *What if human beings did not have tongues?*

"SERIOSITY" is a block to the whole process. Laughter is the key that unlocks divergence. Students need to see and analyze adults using the divergent questioning process. They also need guidance in moving from divergent thinking to convergent thinking.

From **THINKING IS THE KEY-QUESTIONING MAKES THE DIFFERENCE** by Nancy Johnson.
Pieces of Learning 1992.

Questions to Encourage Active Questioners

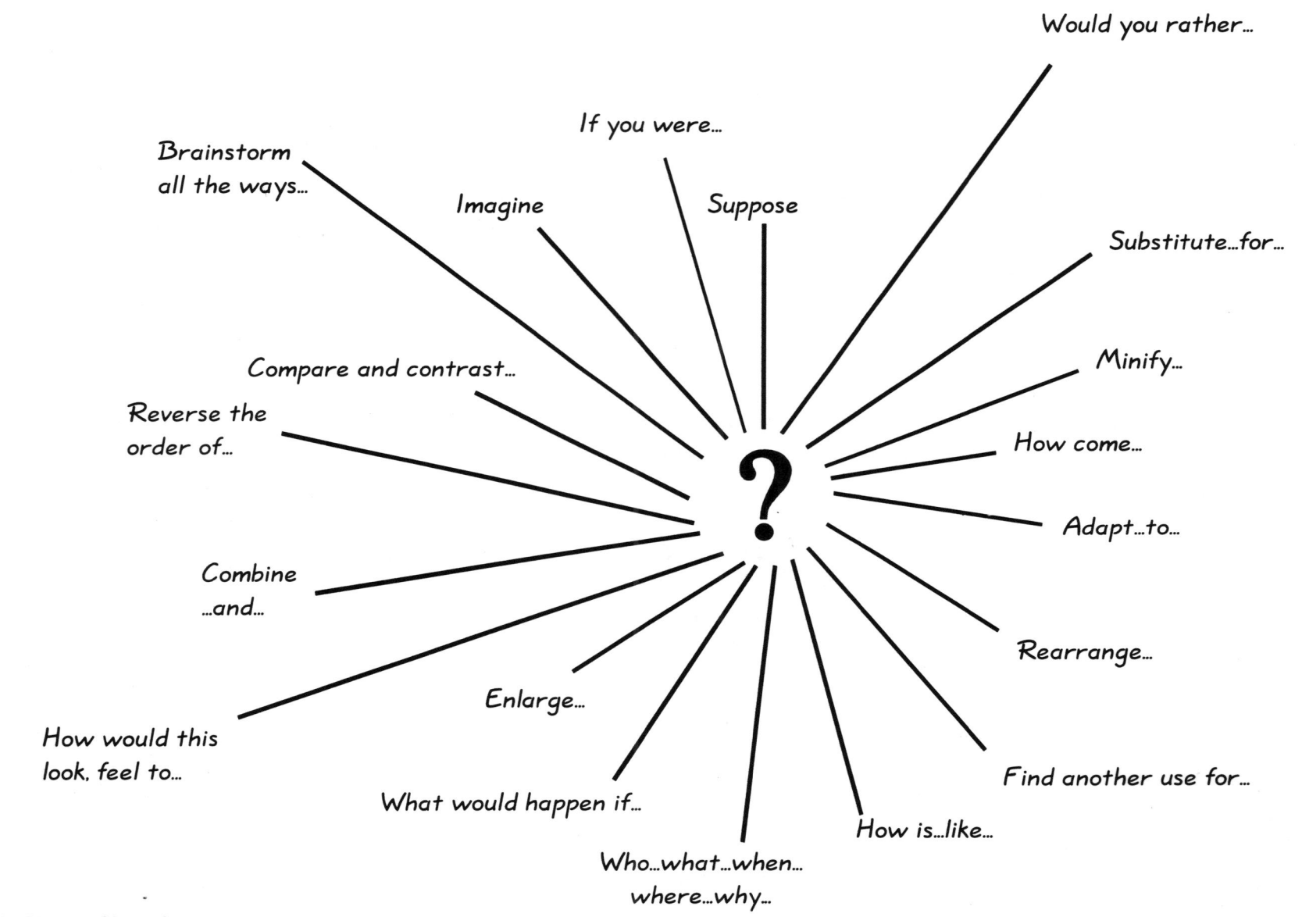

Would you rather...

If you were...

Brainstorm all the ways...

Imagine

Suppose

Substitute...for...

Compare and contrast...

Reverse the order of...

Minify...

How come...

Adapt...to...

Combine ...and...

Rearrange...

Enlarge...

How would this look, feel to...

What would happen if...

Find another use for...

Who...what...when... where...why...

How is...like...

Government Question Web

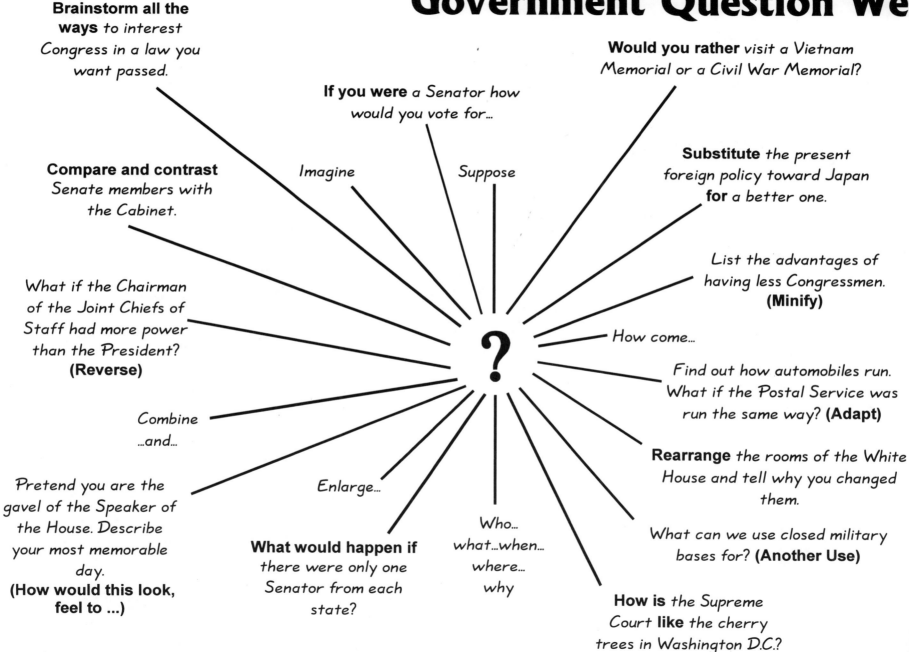

Brainstorm all the **ways** to interest Congress in a law you want passed.

Would you rather visit a Vietnam Memorial or a Civil War Memorial?

If you were a Senator how would you vote for...

Substitute the present foreign policy toward Japan **for** a better one.

Compare and contrast Senate members with the Cabinet.

Imagine

Suppose

List the advantages of having less Congressmen. **(Minify)**

What if the Chairman of the Joint Chiefs of Staff had more power than the President? **(Reverse)**

How come...

Find out how automobiles run. What if the Postal Service was run the same way? **(Adapt)**

Combine ...and...

Rearrange the rooms of the White House and tell why you changed them.

Pretend you are the gavel of the Speaker of the House. Describe your most memorable day. **(How would this look, feel to ...)**

Enlarge...

What can we use closed military bases for? **(Another Use)**

What would happen if there were only one Senator from each state?

Who... what...when... where... why

How is the Supreme Court **like** the cherry trees in Washington D.C.?

Graphic Organizer for Curriculum Development ©

Compare/ Contrast Chart

Invite a foreign exchange student to class to talk about school in Japan.

Would you rather go to an American or Japanese school?

Product

Activity

Question?

Question?

Schools Around the World

Thematic Topic

Activity

Product

What if only Spanish were spoken and written in schools?

Brainstorm ideas. Develop criteria to evaluate best ideas. Select 5 best ideas.

Debate

© Nancy Johnson & Kathy Balsamo 1994

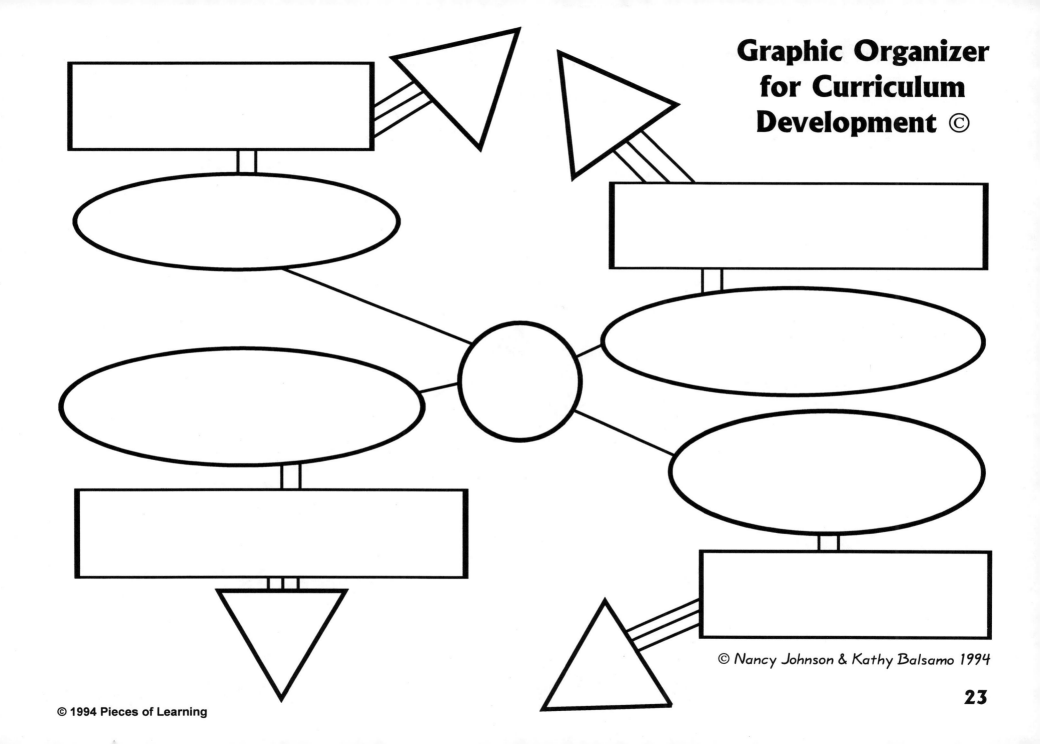

Graphic Organizer for Curriculum Development ©

© Nancy Johnson & Kathy Balsamo 1994

23

Global Education Topics

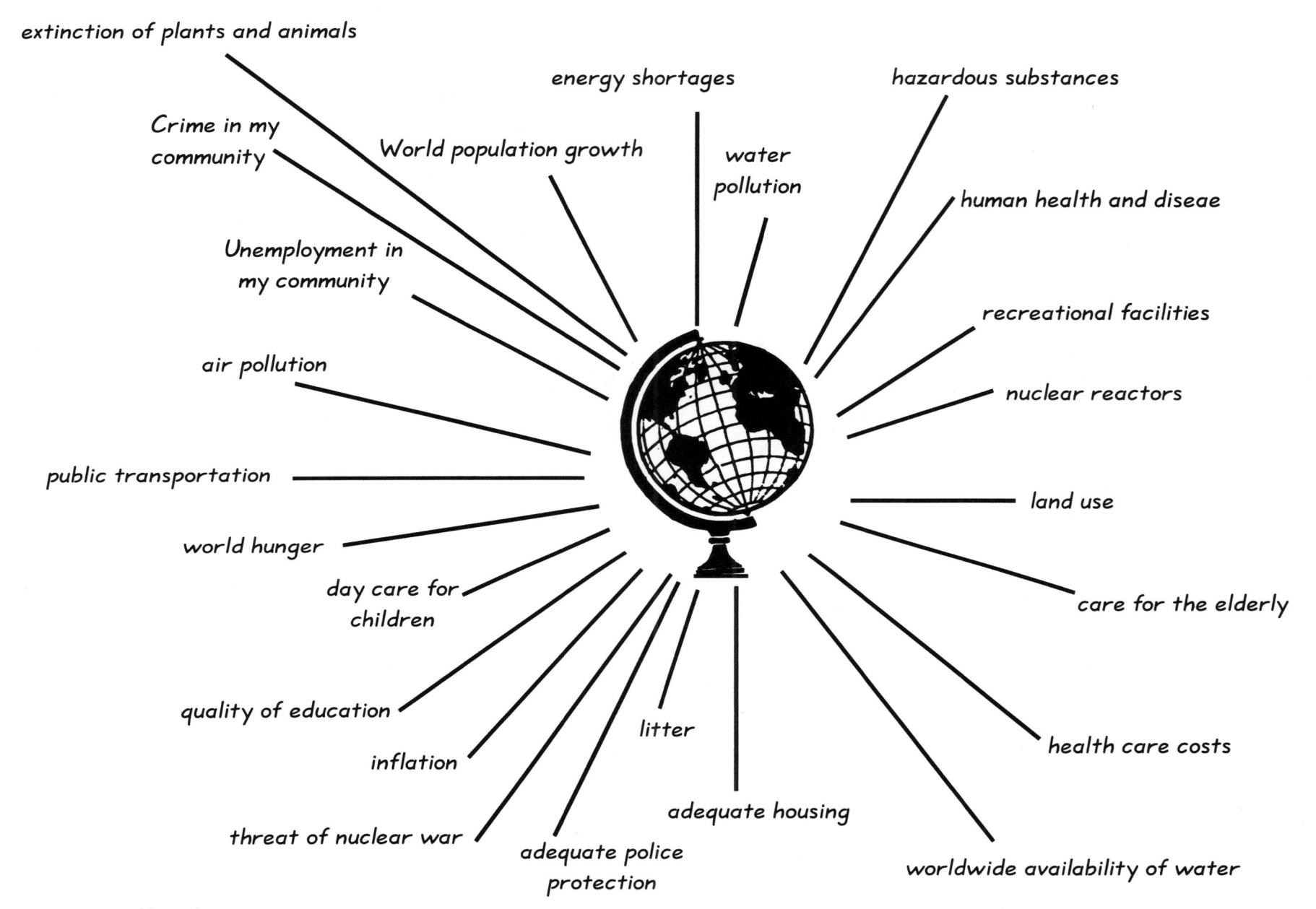

extinction of plants and animals

Crime in my community

World population growth

energy shortages

hazardous substances

water pollution

human health and diseae

Unemployment in my community

recreational facilities

air pollution

nuclear reactors

public transportation

land use

world hunger

day care for children

care for the elderly

quality of education

litter

health care costs

inflation

threat of nuclear war

adequate police protection

adequate housing

worldwide availability of water

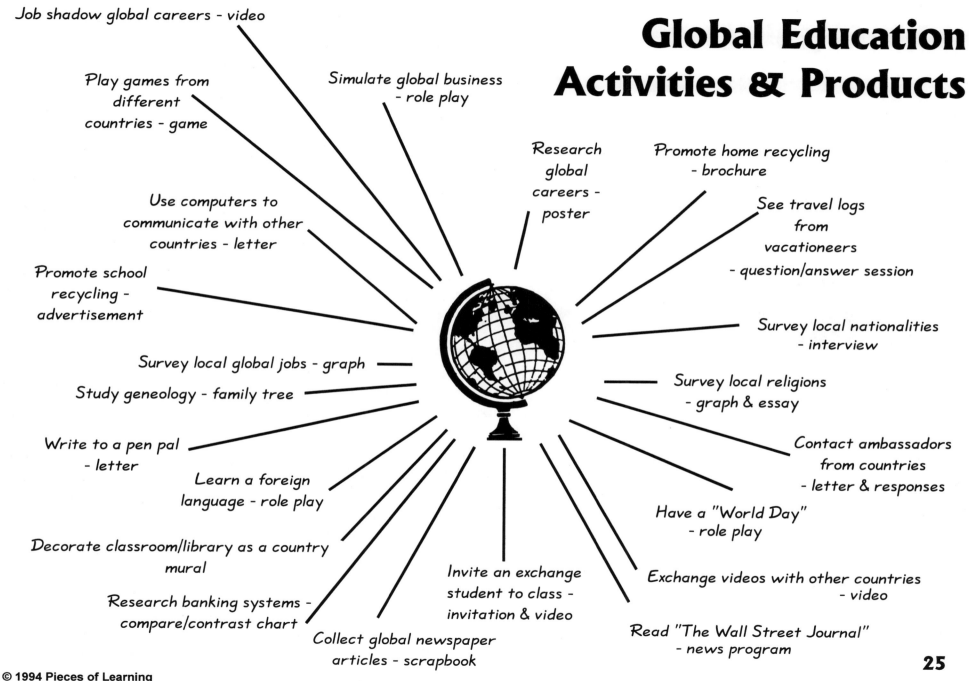

Global Education Activities & Products

Job shadow global careers - video

Play games from different countries - game

Simulate global business - role play

Research global careers - poster

Promote home recycling - brochure

See travel logs from vacationeers - question/answer session

Use computers to communicate with other countries - letter

Promote school recycling - advertisement

Survey local nationalities - interview

Survey local global jobs - graph

Study geneology - family tree

Survey local religions - graph & essay

Write to a pen pal - letter

Learn a foreign language - role play

Contact ambassadors from countries - letter & responses

Decorate classroom/library as a country mural

Have a "World Day" - role play

Research banking systems - compare/contrast chart

Invite an exchange student to class - invitation & video

Exchange videos with other countries - video

Collect global newspaper articles - scrapbook

Read "The Wall Street Journal" - news program

Resources

your own mind
dictionaries
magazines
textbooks
newspapers
almanacs
telephone books
radio
picture books
photographs
maps
graphs
films
filmstrips
encyclopedias
catalogues
computers
television
video tapes
charts
records
tapes
CDs
atlases
Who's Who
your friends
teachers
parents
relatives

neighbors
school workers
city workers
doctors
dentists
professors
scientists
people in careers connected with your
     subject
officers in organizations
Chambers of Commerce
Junior League
Lions Club
university/college teachers
elected officials
library
museum
company
university
newspaper
hospital
walking trip
grocery store
government office
airport
zoo
park
city hall
neighborhood

school year
businesses
television station
radio station
art gallery

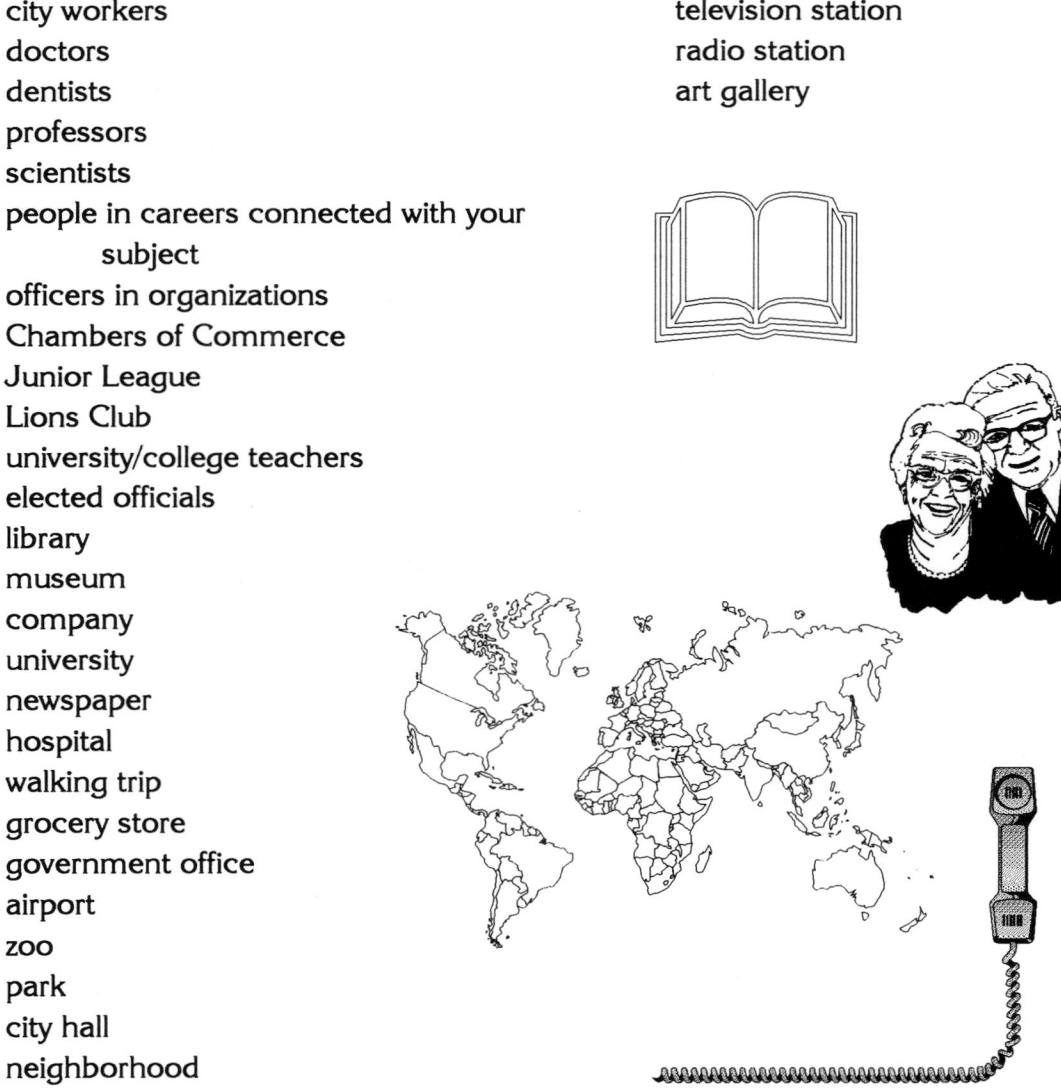

Thematic Units

are motivational because they are

- broad based themes — not focused solely on one content area to the exclusion of all others
- often student initiated concepts that begin with student and teacher questions and then are teacher-directed based on the theme
- integrated and provide for enrichment—telescoping, postholing, differentiation
- opportunities for academic AND attitude assessment - positive, cooperative, inquisitive, tolerant, open-minded, risk-taking
- objective oriented (See P. 28)
- opportunities for high level thinking skills, research, "new techniques or materials", more than "right" answers with products that answer the problem or issue with appropriate audiences

SCIENCE - Investigate the teeth of the beaver and the necessity for gnawing. Investigate other structural adaptations such as the inability to breathe through the mouth, valves in the ears and nose, and its life in the water. Name other adaptions of animals and man.

SOCIAL STUDIES - Compare Indian and white man's need for the beaver and compare and contrast their conservation practices. What would happen if beavers became extinct? How would their extinction affect the land? Man?

MUSIC - Investigate sounds made by the beaver, pond sounds, and forest sounds. Recreate the sounds with musical instruments. Why are these kinds of sounds thought to be relazing?

ART - Draw a cross section of a beaver lodge and label. Make a mural of a beaver pond. Make life-size papier mache or clay beavers. Are there other animals that live like the beaver?

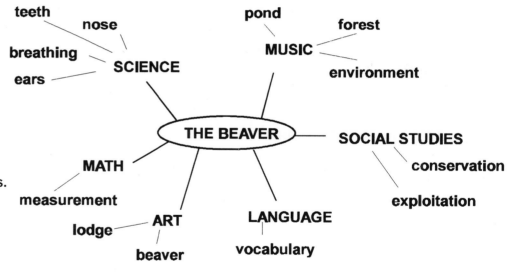

LANGUAGE - Read from **The Tales of Hiawatha** *"The Hunting of Pau-Puk Keewis."* Write a guided imagery of a beaver building a dam. List words that are peculiar to a beaver's world.

MATH - Discover the beaver length in inches and centimeters; the beaver weight in pounds and kilograms; the dam length in feet and meters; how fast a beaver can swim in miles per hour and kilometers.

- from *It's About Writing* by Kathy Balsamo, *Pieces of Learning*

© 1994 Pieces of Learning

27

Learner Outcomes and Unit Objectives

LEARNER OUTCOMES

The student will . . .

1. demonstrate the capacity to **apply, analyze, synthesize and evaluate** printed materials to accomplish written exercises.
2. demonstrate an ability to undertake library research in order to **gather data** for the completion of assignments.
3. **exhibit fluency** by producing ideas by citing multiple responses in those activities calling for large numbers of responses.
4. evidence an ability to **interact easily** with others by readily participating in the planned group activities.
5. demonstrate an ability to **use social skills** in participating in group activities.
6. demonstrate an ability to **articulate ideas** clearly during the group activities.
7. demonstrate the ability to **use acceptable grammar and punctuation** in writing.
8. **demonstrate organizational ability** through the completion of an acceptable written composition.
9. show an ability to **recognize** the skills and abilities of **others** by sharing products and abilities and reinforcing the efforts of peers.
10. **depict visually** two remote or commonly disassociated ideas.
11. demonstrate an ability to **redefine elements of a task** by moving sequentially from the generation and selection of items to the successful completion of a product.

12. develop a more positive self-concept by **recognizing and using abilities, becoming more self-directed, and appreciating likenesses and differences** between himself and others.
13. **develop ideas** related to broad-based issues, themes, or problems.
14. be involved in an **in-depth learning experience** related to a self-directed topic.
15. **generate original ideas** in completing a model, plan, picture, dance or other product that is unique.
16. show ability to recognize goals and objectives of a group by **working toward consensus** in planned group activities.
17. produce many pictures/movements to **make comparisons** among things, show relationships or associations.
18. effectively **interpret** and use nonverbal forms of communication to **express** ideas, feelings, and needs to others.
19. use a variety of pictures/movements to **describe feelings and values.**
20. **predict** many different causes/effects of given situations through the use of pictures and movement.
21. express a variety of kinds of responses. **(Flexibility)**
22. express unusual, uncommon responses, though not all of the ideas prove to be useful. **(Originality)**
23. build into or embellish a basic idea by adding details to make it more interesting and complete. **(Elaboration)**

Guidelines for Developing Units

Design thematic units to develop thinking skills. Emphasize the following teaching strategies:

1. Help the learners to probe a *subject in depth.*

2. Provide an opportunity to *utilize higher-level thought processes* on a regular basis, especially divergent-evaluative thinking.

3. Assist learners in *demonstrating self-motivation* in some discipline.

4. Provide, on a regular basis, multiple opportunities to *be creative.*

5. Provide an educational framework within which students can challenge and *stimulate each other* and share learning experiences designed to help them use their talents productively.

6. Provide multiple *opportunities for self-expression.*

7. Provide opportunities for learners to *demonstrate perseverance* in the face of obstacles.

8. Assist learners to *master research skills* for independence and discovery.

9. Assist learners to *assume responsibility* for their own learning.

10. Reduce the amount of teacher talk—lectures. Increase *student inquiry talking—interaction.*

11. Insist on *using multi resources* in the study of the unit, using books and numerous other types of references.

12. Include *evaluative techniques* as part of the original unit.

13. *Encourage "hidden talent"* to reveal itself during regular class time.

14. Provide *sequential activities* progressing from lower level learning activities to high level activities.

—*Learning Outcomes and Guidelines for Developing Units from* **The BEST Teacher 'STUFF'** *by Nancy Johnson, Pieces of Learning, 1993 Developing Units adapted from LTI consultant Dr. Sandra Kaplan*

The 90s' students are visual and often random learners. Therefore, webbing is a natural process for them. Webbing is one kind of graphic organizer. Use it to determine all the possible directions a student can go (questions), all the activities a student can do to explore a theme and all the possible products to produce. In student portfolios, use the web to assess student interests, show works in progress, and show finished products.

Goals for Students in Thematic Webbing —

to stimulate thinking and asking questions

to take ownership of their learning

to learn to locate and use multiple resources

to connect curriculum areas to each other

to ask questions to explore possibilities that extend study into new areas

and . . . Students will . . .

Assume responsibility for their learning

Practice making decisions

Practice problem solving

Learn to evaluate by developing criteria

Learn to interact, cooperate, and work as a group member while developing as an individual

Learn to share and discuss problems and successes

The Webbing Experience

Webbing Skills

1. Thinking Skills: think divergently; hold judgment on ideas
2. Process Skills: Locate, collect information from multiple resources
                          Organize information and manipulate ideas from random to sequential on a graphic organizer
                          Evaluate information

Webbing is a great **graphic organizer** to help students investigate a thematic unit and to use as motivators for independent study and enrichment projects. Before beginning a thematic study brainstorm with the class what they know about a subject. Write all the words and phrases they know in web form.

Example — On the next page **"Bodyworks"** is an example of a theme in a graphic organizer. It randomly generated 10 question/activity/product areas. One area **INSTRUMENTS** was webbed further brainstorming only questions. Any of the ideas can be further brainstormed with student questions and suggestions for activities and products. Once the web is complete, individual students, partners, and/or cooperative groups can choose questions, activities, and products to pursue.

✳ *IDEA Spray "Spray Mount" on the back of the webbed page. Cut out individual activities and make a "Wall Web." Students can add to the Wall Web by writing additional questions and activities and products on post notes and sticking them to the Wall. (A removable Wall or table web). After all ideas are placed, individual students, partners, and/or cooperative groups can choose (remove from the Wall Web) questions, activities, and products to pursue.*

Add to the web as the students learn new terms and concepts. Develop learning centers to complement the study. Glue individual webs in folders. As each activity is completed have the student check it off on the web and decide if it is to be selected for inclusion in the portfolio.

Bodyworks

Who was its inventor?

What does it tell you?

How expensive is it to use?

Who is certified to use it?

Make a list of instruments used to check your health.

List all the ways to check your health without using an instrument.

Interview active senior citizens in their homes or retirement villages. Find out why they are "physically fit." Use video, audio, or chart responses.

With a partner make up rules and trivia questions for a game called "Bodyworks."

Choose one. Compare & contrast old and new versions.

What would happen if there were no thermometers?

What would a stethoscope say to a beating heart?

Write and try recipes for a cookbook with special sections for
-young children -teachers
-teenagers -grandparents
-parents
Bring them to school to taste. Make and sell the cookbook as a fund-raiser.

Is it a preventive or diagnostic?

Would you rather be an inventor of an instrument or the one who uses it? Why?

Choose 2 instruments. List attributes of both. Combine attributes to make a new instrument. Name it. What does it do?

In a small group design a poster of food groups necessary for good health. Bring examples to share with group members.

Make a chart of selected diseases, their symptoms, their causes, their diagnoses and their prescriptions.

Make a model lung. Or pretend you are a lung. Write and give a dialog between the left and right lung—the heart and a lung—the brain and a lung.

Report on Louis Pasteur. Compare and contrast his discovery to Jonas Salk's discovery. What if milk was not pasteurized today? List food items that need to be sterilized and tell why.

Create a collage of products people use to change their appearances. What are good reasons to change appearance? What thing would you change about yourself? Why?

Survey 5 students. How many heartbeats per minute? Graph results. What is the average? Is it better to have a high or low heartbeat? Why?

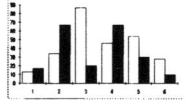

Portfolios

Portfolios are NOT

✘ work folders   ✘ random accumulations of work   ✘ workbook pages

✘ samples of acquired facts   ✘ samples of what the student CANNOT do

Portfolios ARE authentic assessment of what a student can do over a period of time. They

- are collected *and* spontaneous examples of work;
- are student-centered;
- encourage student responsibility.

Students are compared to themselves. Thus they can establish attainable goals for themselves by realistically assessing their achievement or lack of achievement of attitudes, concepts, and skills. Using portfolios students observe their academic and affective growth, understand how they feel about process and content, and determine their strengths and weaknesses.

Portfolios ARE:

✔ products that are examples of process, curriculum integration, **and** achievement.

✔ products of individual as well as cooperative work.

✔ examples of

    talents   preferred learning style   interests   strengths.

✔ relative/comparative amounts of effort.

✔ reflections of a student's changes in or consistency of thought, motivation, attitudes, and flexibility.

� Portfolios encourage life long learning skills and the 3Rs for the 21st Century (P. 9):

- self assessment
- creative thinking skill components (fluency, flexibility, elaboration, originality, risk-taking)
- critical thinking skills
- cooperative group skills--people skills

Portfolios encourage a variety of assessment:

Affective skills

- Content interest inventory
- Learning styles inventory
- Peer assessment/evaluation of cooperative work skills
- Adult assessment/evaluation of motivation, cooperative work skills, and attitudes
- Skills inventory
- Self assessment/evaluation of motivation
- Self assessment/evaluation of attitudes

Academic Skills

- Content assessment/evaluation: subjective and objective
- Self assessment/evaluation of product
- Adult assessment/evaluation of product
- Peer assessment/evaluation of product
- Self assessment/evaluation of process
- Adult assessment/evaluation of process

Sample Criteria for Product Assessment:

- Organization
- Clarity
- Relatedness
- Grammar
- Detail
- Appropriateness
- Level of expectation

Possible Criteria for Process Assessment (Rating Scale)

- Knowledge - how well do I know. . .
- Comprehension - how well do I understand. . .
- Application - how can I apply this to. . .
- Analysis - how well can I "take apart" the parts. . .
- Synthesis - how well can I "put together" parts to make. . .
- Evaluation - how well can I determine criteria to evaluate. . .

❃ Compared to What?

It's easy to assess handwriting! Just compare it to the chart provided by the textbook company! But what about an essay? a cartoon? a skit? The key—not the answer—is to establish assessment/evaluation criteria BEFORE the activity and product are chosen. A "poor" artist may not choose a cartoon to depict the sequence of a story if she is a better writer. Likewise a "poor" writer will not choose an essay if he is a better speaker. A skit with a partner may be better for him. And a shy child may choose not to present a skit in front of the class.

Remember also in a portfolio are examples of attempts at different styles and different products that may be assessed but not graded. Discuss with the student prior to activity and product choice if the process and product are being ASSESSED or EVALUATED and what the levels of expectation are.

If portfolio content is generated during thematic units, besides final products the portfolio may include photos of products; student awards for completion or competition; written samples including mindmaps, edited first drafts, outlines; audio tapes of "thinking out loud"; resources such as charts, graphs, logs, journals, book lists; self observations, reflections, and evaluations; videotape, computer-generated products, samples of group work, a transparency, audio of panel discussion or debate, time line or flow chart that can . . .

analyze	find examples	solve
appraise	generalize	summarize
contrast	hypothesize	show
combine	illustrate	sequence
classify	initiate	substitute
categorize	improve	translate
compose	imagine	take apart
construct	identify	
change	invent	
compare	judge	
criticize	justify	
demonstrate	label	
design	modify	
defend	organize	
dissect	propose	
explain	relate	
evaluate	restructure	
forecast	recommend	

✱ Since not everything can go into a portfolio, students must develop criteria to select and assess products that will be included. Developing and selecting criteria is a life long learning skill in itself. As criteria is refined, that problem solving skill improves.

Criteria for Assessment of Products for Student Portfolios

A Sample

Sliding Scale

	1	2	3	4	5
1. Organization					
2. Clarity of thought/thinking skills used					
3. Product follows-through assignment					
4. Form—Grammatically correct					
5. Thoroughness (appropriately focused on the topic selected)					
6. Resources					
7. Management of time					
8. Task orientation					
9. Understanding—generalizations, interpretations, conclusions					
10. Creativity					
11. Quality of presentation					

Report / Audio - Print - Video

1. Well organized introduction, body, conclusion
2. Details support hypothesis or each idea
3. Grammatically correct
4. Factually accurate

Time Line

1. Chronologically accurate
2. Important facts indicated (application)
3. Well-plotted time spans

Sliding Scale

	1	2	3	4	5

Poem / Story / Lyrics

1. Clarity of thought - theme easily identifiable (beginning, body, end) . . . .
2. Grammatically correct . . . .
3. Creativity . . . .

Journal

1. Elements identifiable . . . .
2. Accuracy of information . . . .
3. Grammatically correct . . . .

Magazine/newspaper article

1. Grammatically correct . . . .
2. Factually accurate . . . .
3. Includes who, what, when, where, why, how . . . .
4. Quality of 1st sentence as a "grabber" . . . .
5. Conciseness . . . .

Flipbook - also see story

1. Artwork complements story elements in importance and time . . . .
2. Includes artwork that illustrates who, what, where, when, why, how . . . .
3. Accuracy of sequence . . . .

Dictionary

1. Alphabetically accurate . . . .
2. Grammatically correct . . . .
3. Appropriate words chosen . . . .
4. Accuracy of definition . . . .

	1	2	3	4	5

List

    1. Adequate length   . . . .

    2. Relates to topic at hand   . . . .

Brochure/Booklet/Pamphlet

    1. Conciseness   . . . .

    2. Grammatically correct   . . . .

    3. Well-organized   . . . .

    4. Attractiveness   . . . .

Trivia game

    1. Appropriate questions   . . . .

    2. Adequate number of questions   . . . .

    3. Accuracy of answers   . . . .

    4. Quality of game board   . . . .

    5. Clarity of rules   . . . .

    6. Originality   . . . .

Letter / essay / editorial / debate

    1. Author's point of view/opinion is clear   . . . .

    2. The point of view/opinion is supported by details   . . . .

    3. Grammatically correct   . . . .

    4. Flowing sequence of ideas presented   . . . .

Map

    1. Map information relates directly to assignment   . . . .

    2. Well-organized (written or verbal)   . . . .

    3. Grammatically correct explanation of the map   . . . .

    4. Well-organized, clearly & accurately labeled map   . . . .

Sliding Scale

	1	2	3	4	5

Survey / Graph / Chart

1. Appropriate visual (chart or graph)
2. Appropriate questions
3. Appropriateness of title and descriptors
4. Correctness of information charted or graphed
5. Deductive reasoning used to make conclusions from the graph/chart
6. Grammatically correct statements
7. Well-organized

Quiz / Crossword Puzzle

1. Importance of questions
2. Variety of questions
3. Grammatically correct
4. Accuracy of answers

Guiness Book

1. Clarity of thought
2. Paragraph has topic sentence, main idea, supporting details
3. Includes who, what, when, where
4. Grammatically correct

Drama / Pantomime / Video

1. Flow of presentation (preparation)
2. Accuracy of information related
3. Resources cited

Mural / Drawing / Poster / Model / Mobile / Diorama / Collage

1. Neatness
2. Accuracy applied from information used
3. Resources cited

Teacher Assessment Criteria for Process/Products/Projects ⁴⁰

Compared to What?
Compared to the teacher's experience with this student and other students. Discuss criteria with the student.

	1	2	3	4	5

To what extent . . .

— did the student appropriately focus, narrow, broaden the topic being examined?

— did the student clearly define the topic being examined?

— has the student used more than a single source of information in gathering data for the project?

— were the sources of information the student used appropriate for the topic?

— did the student appropriately paraphrase the information gathered in making the final presentation?

— has the student appropriately synthesized the data collected and presented it in a meaningful "whole"?

— did the student make appropriate generalizations on the basis of the information presented?

— did the student make appropriate interpretations of the information gathered?

— did the student present appropriate concluding or summary statements of the information presented?

— did the product seem to reflect the student's real interest in the topic?

Student Assessment Criteria

Compared to What?
Compared to the student's experience with this activity and other activities.

	1	2	3	4	5
1. Enjoyment, pride, satisfaction of process and product					
2. Independence of ideas and efforts					
3. Commitment to project					
4. Product quality					
5. Knowledge gained					

Attitude
Consideration toward others . . . .

Cooperative . . . .

Interest . . . .

Participation
Works without direction . . . .

Management of time . . . .

Responsible . . . .

Leadership . . . .

Problem Solving
Recognizes problem . . . .

Asks question to define and defines problem . . . .

Formulates and states hypothesis . . . .

Plans procedure to test hypothesis . . . .

Collects and records, tabulates data . . . .

Organizes data in meaningful way(product) . . . .

More Activities
Bodyworks

Make a poster or collage showing people expressing different emotions.

Survey people's favorite snacks. Graph results.

Make a wordfind of "Good Foods."

Trace around your body and label as many parts as you can.

Make a scrapbook of current events in the health field.

Mindmap careers that have to do with "Bodyworks."

What if we had no muscles? Write 10 consequences.

List 10 ways germs spread. For each list ways to prevent that kind of spreading.

You are a red blood cell. Describe your round trip body journey.

Which is more important — having two lungs or two kidneys? Why?

Make a Guiness Book of "Body Records."

Diagram each body system. Use transparencies and overlay the systems on the body outline on the overhead projector. Describe the necessity of each system to the class.

Compare / contrast brains and computers. What are the advantages of brains?

Sample

Portfolio Activity   42

Name Mary, Nancy   **Thematic Unit** Bodyworks

Make a model lung. Write and give a dialog between the left and right lung.

Objective To apply knowledge and generate original ideas in completing a model

Learning Style(s) kinesthetic/verbal/concrete random

Product(s) model / written & verbal dialog

Assessment Criteria	1	2	3	4	5
Organization			✔		
Clarity of thought					✔
Process follow-through			✔		
Grammar					✔
Thoroughness				✔	
Resources	filmstrip, science book, American Lung Association				
Time Management			✔		
Understanding				✔	
Creativity				✔	
Quality of Presentation				✔	

Comments: The lungs were made from plastic that Mary and Nancy wore. Then they conversed with each other as right and left lung to tell functions. Worked well together.

Content Areas ☐ Math ✔ English ☐ Reading ✔ Art ☐ Social Studies ✔ Science ☐ Music ☐

Activities

Portfolio Activity

Name _____

Date   **Thematic Unit** _____

Activity _____

_____

_____

_____

Objective _____

Learning Style(s) _____

Product(s) _____

Assessment Criteria	1	2	3	4	5
Organization					
Clarity of thought					
Process follow-through					
Grammar					
Thoroughness					
Resources					
Time Management					
Understanding					
Creativity					
Quality of Presentation					

_____

_____

_____

_____

_____

Content Areas

☐ Math ☐ English ☐ Reading ☐ Art ☐ Social Studies ☐ Science
☐ Music ☐ _____

Student Inventory

Preferred Learning Style Descriptors

_____
_____
_____
_____

Preferred Verbs p. 14

_____
_____
_____
_____

Preferred Activities p. 15

_____
_____
_____
_____

Preferred Activities p. 16

_____
_____
_____
_____
_____
_____
_____

Preferred Products p. 17

_____
_____
_____
_____
_____
_____
_____

Activities to Try p. 16

1. _____

2. _____

3. _____

4. _____

5. _____

6. _____

Products to Try p. 17

1. _____

2. _____

3. _____

4. _____

5. _____

6. _____

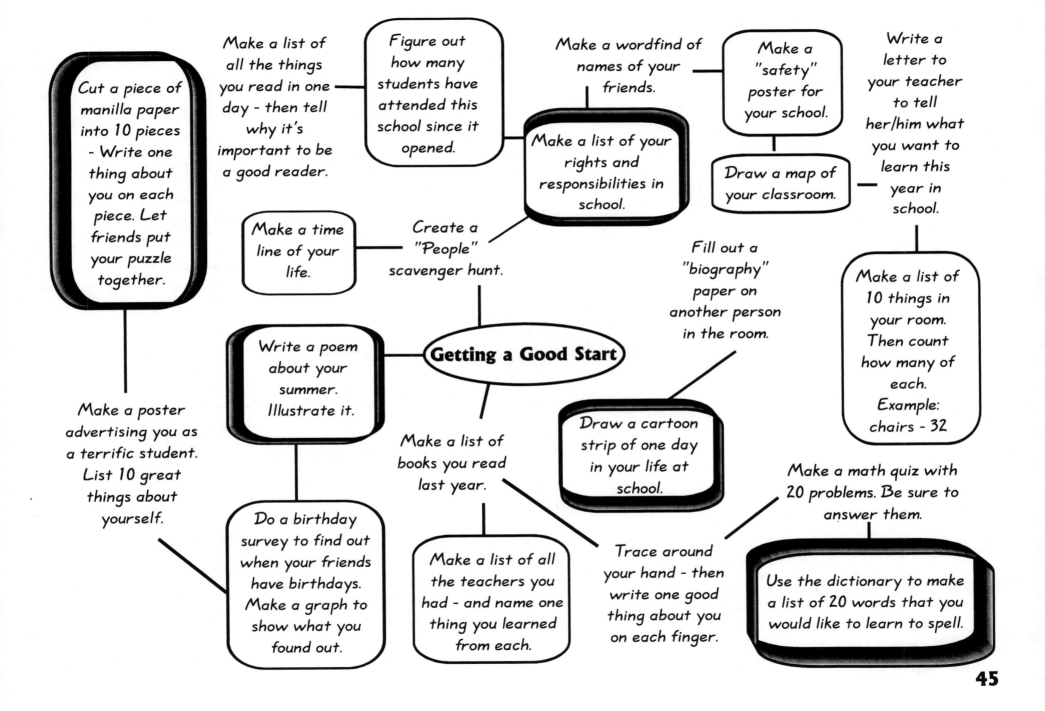

Cut a piece of manilla paper into 10 pieces - Write one thing about you on each piece. Let friends put your puzzle together.

Make a list of all the things you read in one day - then tell why it's important to be a good reader.

Figure out how many students have attended this school since it opened.

Make a wordfind of names of your friends.

Make a "safety" poster for your school.

Write a letter to your teacher to tell her/him what you want to learn this year in school.

Make a list of your rights and responsibilities in school.

Draw a map of your classroom.

Make a time line of your life.

Create a "People" scavenger hunt.

Fill out a "biography" paper on another person in the room.

Make a list of 10 things in your room. Then count how many of each. Example: chairs - 32

Getting a Good Start

Write a poem about your summer. Illustrate it.

Make a poster advertising you as a terrific student. List 10 great things about yourself.

Do a birthday survey to find out when your friends have birthdays. Make a graph to show what you found out.

Make a list of books you read last year.

Draw a cartoon strip of one day in your life at school.

Make a math quiz with 20 problems. Be sure to answer them.

Make a list of all the teachers you had - and name one thing you learned from each.

Trace around your hand - then write one good thing about you on each finger.

Use the dictionary to make a list of 20 words that you would like to learn to spell.

45

Animals

Make an animal dictionary. Illustrate with magazine cutouts.

Make an Animal Riddle Book.

What animals have been important in US history? Explain why.

Choose a zoo animal that also lives in the wild. Make a time line of both of their lives.

Make a list of vertebrates and invertebrates found in the zoo.

Compare and contrast African and Asian elephants.

What makes a skunk smell?

Write a script between a dog catcher and a vagabond dog.

Put together a scrapbook of different breeds of an animal. Explain how they are different.

What would a cougar in the wild ask a cougar in the zoo?

Make a bar graph to show how long selected animals live. Write 5 facts you can deduce from the graph.

Why do cats have whiskers? Name other animals that have whiskers.

Write a newspaper article about a wild animal found in your state.

Play Animal Charades. Pantomime an animal's behaviors and movements. Have classmates identify the animal.

Build a bird feeder and make a list of the birds that might come to your feeder. Why will they come?

Paint a mural of a beaver home and its surroundings.

More Activities
Animals

Create a set of 10 Animal Trivia cards.

Make a Guiness Book of Animal Records.

Write a report on primates and list the ones in a zoo.

Report on and illustrate the raccoon.

What are mammals? Make a web of the zoo mammals.

Design a "Be Kind to Animals" poster.

What's the difference between a crocodile and an alligator? Illustrate and label.

What are the laws in your county about having a dog?

List ways dogs help man. List other animals that help man.

Make a poster of wild animal homes found in your state.

Draw a pet parade.

Make a book about an animal you would like to be.

Design a chart showing the kinds of freshwater fish found in your state.

Make an animal wordfind or crossword puzzle.

Portfolio Activity

Name _____

Date _____ **Thematic Unit** _____

Activity _____

_____

_____

_____

Objective _____

Learning Style(s) _____

Product(s) _____

Assessment Criteria	1	2	3	4	5
Organization					
Clarity of thought					
Process follow-through					
Grammar					
Thoroughness					
Resources					
Time Management					
Understanding					
Creativity					
Quality of Presentation					

_____

_____

_____

_____

Content Areas

☐ Math ☐ English ☐ Reading ☐ Art ☐ Social Studies ☐ Science
☐ Music ☐ _____

Backyard Beasties

Create a game that will teach facts about "Backyard Beasties."

How do plagues of insects affect a population? What happens to the people? Give examples.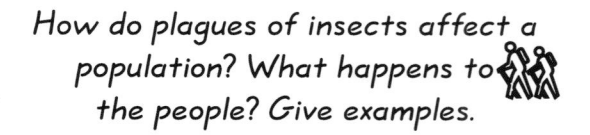

Write an article for a newspaper telling why a certain insect is needed.

Classify biting and non-biting insects.

Construct an insect's "house."

Create a mobile with facts about insects.

With a partner interview insects. Ask them to tell and show how they protect themselves.

How do bats, birds, and frogs catch insects? Pretend you are an insect. Persuade the bat, bird or frog not to catch you. Give at least 3 reasons.

Make an insect cartoon character and write a cartoon strip.

Brainstorm all the songs you know about insects. Then write lyrics about a helpful insect using the melody of a song you know.

Make a roller movie about life in an ant hill or bee hive.

Use a map of the US to show where harmful regional insects live.

Write a report about spider webs. Tell how they are made, what they are used for, and illustrate a typical web.

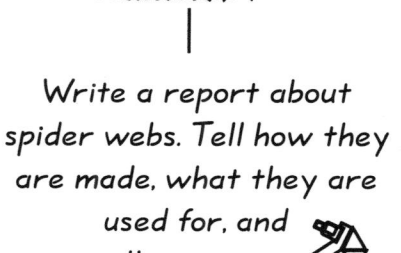

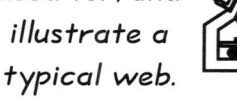

Take a survey. Tabulate results and make a graph of your classmate's favorite insects. Write 5 facts you can deduce from the graph.

More Activities
Backyard Beasties

Create a book cover to tell about your favorite insect.

Make a wordfind of 20 insects.

Write a poem about an insect.

Make a chart of the 4 stages of metamorphosis.

Create 10 Insect Trivia cards.

Compare these backyard beasties: insects, spiders, centipedes, millipedes.

What is entomology?

Why does a firefly light up?

How do beekeepers take care of bees?

Design a poster showing insect homes.

What are arachnids? Make a list and illustrate.

Design a booklet of harmful and helpful mini-beasts.

Draw 4 differenct insects and label their parts.

Collect insects. Observe them & record your findings.

Compare the life cycles of a butterfly, moth, grasshopper and mosquito.

What is a compound eye? Show how it works.

Where do insects go in winter? What do they do?

Portfolio Activity

Name _____

Date _____ **Thematic Unit** _____

Activity _____

_____

_____

Objective _____

Learning Style(s) _____

Product(s) _____

Assessment Criteria	1	2	3	4	5
Organization					
Clarity of thought					
Process follow-through					
Grammar					
Thoroughness					
Resources					
Time Management					
Understanding					
Creativity					
Quality of Presentation					

_____

_____

_____

_____

_____

Content Areas

☐ Math ☐ English ☐ Reading ☐ Art ☐ Social Studies ☐ Science
☐ Music ☐ _____

Bodyworks

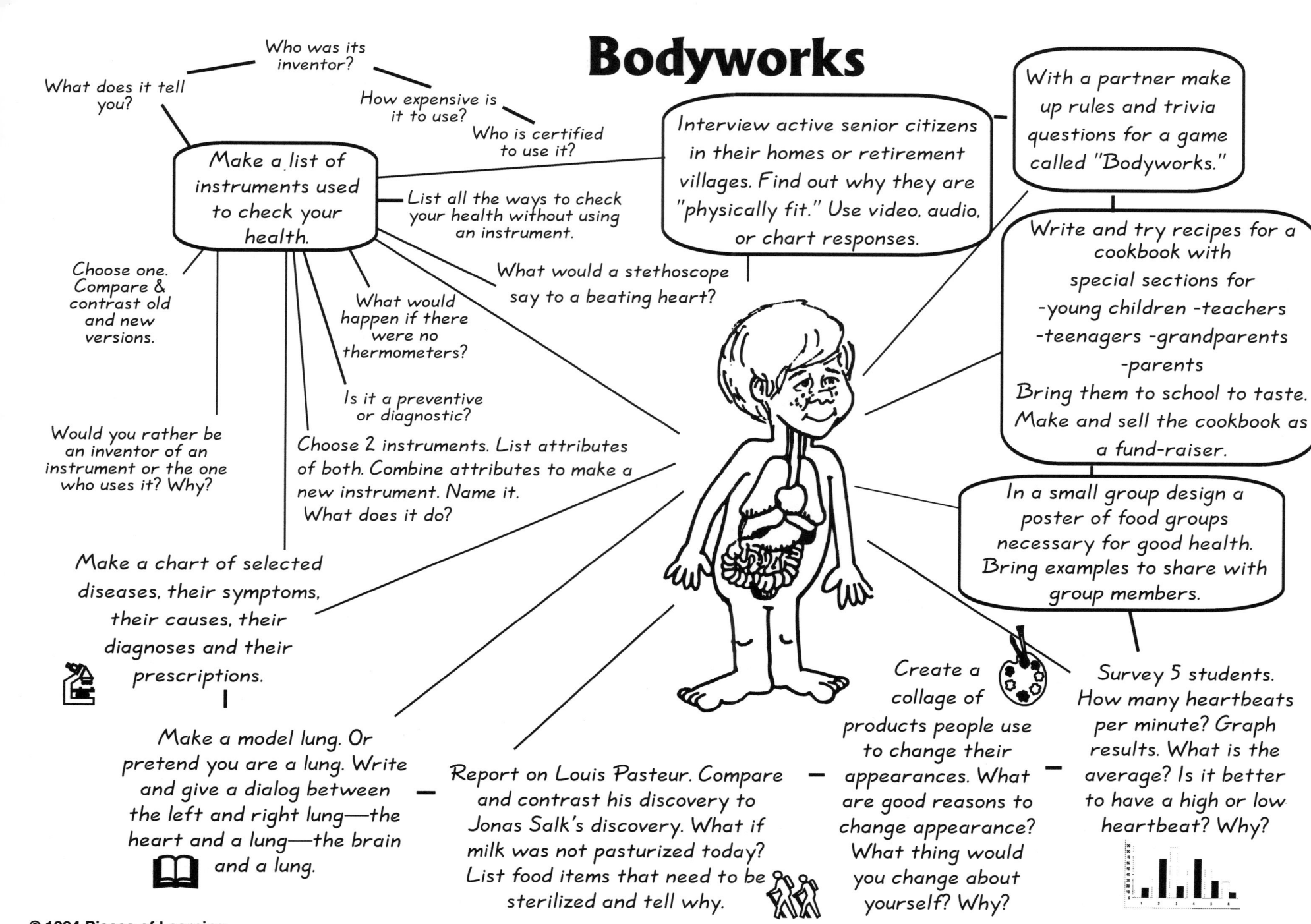

Who was its inventor?

What does it tell you?

How expensive is it to use?

Who is certified to use it?

Make a list of instruments used to check your health.

List all the ways to check your health without using an instrument.

Interview active senior citizens in their homes or retirement villages. Find out why they are "physically fit." Use video, audio, or chart responses.

With a partner make up rules and trivia questions for a game called "Bodyworks."

Choose one. Compare & contrast old and new versions.

What would happen if there were no thermometers?

What would a stethoscope say to a beating heart?

Write and try recipes for a cookbook with special sections for
-young children -teachers
-teenagers -grandparents
-parents
Bring them to school to taste. Make and sell the cookbook as a fund-raiser.

Would you rather be an inventor of an instrument or the one who uses it? Why?

Is it a preventive or diagnostic?

Choose 2 instruments. List attributes of both. Combine attributes to make a new instrument. Name it. What does it do?

In a small group design a poster of food groups necessary for good health. Bring examples to share with group members.

Make a chart of selected diseases, their symptoms, their causes, their diagnoses and their prescriptions.

Make a model lung. Or pretend you are a lung. Write and give a dialog between the left and right lung—the heart and a lung—the brain and a lung.

Report on Louis Pasteur. Compare and contrast his discovery to Jonas Salk's discovery. What if milk was not pasturized today? List food items that need to be sterilized and tell why.

Create a collage of products people use to change their appearances. What are good reasons to change appearance? What thing would you change about yourself? Why?

Survey 5 students. How many heartbeats per minute? Graph results. What is the average? Is it better to have a high or low heartbeat? Why?

More Activities
Bodyworks

Make a poster or collage showing people expressing different emotions.

Survey people's favorite snacks. Graph results.

Make a wordfind of "Good Foods."

Trace around your body and label as many parts as you can.

Make a scrapbook of current events in the health field.

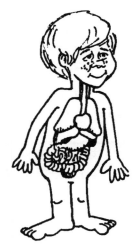

Mindmap careers that have to do with "Bodyworks."

What if we had no muscles? Write 10 consequences.

List 10 ways germs spread. For each list ways to prevent that kind of spreading.

You are a red blood cell. Describe your roundtrip body journey.

Which is more important — having two lungs or two kidneys? Why?

Make a Guiness Book of "Body Records."

Diagram each body system. Use transparencies and overlay the systems on the body outline on the overhead projector. Describe the necessity of each system to the class.

Portfolio Activity

Name _____

Date _____ Thematic Unit _____

Activity _____

_____

_____

Objective _____

Learning Style(s) _____

Product(s) _____

Assessment Criteria	1	2	3	4	5
Organization					
Clarity of thought					
Process follow-through					
Grammar					
Thoroughness					
Resources					
Time Management					
Understanding					
Creativity					
Quality of Presentation					

_____

_____

_____

_____

_____

Content Areas

☐ Math ☐ English ☐ Reading ☐ Art ☐ Social Studies ☐ Science
☐ Music ☐ _____

The World of Dinosaurs

Make a life-size mural of a dinosaur. List facts and myths on the dinosaur skin.

How would you trap a dinosaur?

Make a dinosaur family tree.

Make an illustrated compare/contrast chart to show the differences among the wings of a pterosaur, a bird, and a bat. Write 5 facts you can deduce from your chart.

Design a gameboard for a game called "Digging for Dinosaurs". Create game rules with players as different dinosaurs and play with a partner.

What would happen if a tiny dinosaur followed you home from school?

Make clay models of fossils. Identify each by name and tell what other animals lived with that animal.

From the ceiling hang a time line of the history of the dinosaurs.

Make a paper mache flying reptile. Explain to the class its history.

Construct a dinosaur diorama.

On a map of the world label where dinosaurs lived. Identify the kinds of dinosaurs.

Make a time line to show how a sea animal becomes a fossil.

Would you rather live when the dinosaurs did or in the year 3000? Write an essay telling your reasons.

Lay out the front page of a newspaper. Write news stories and feature stories about the discovery of a dinosaur fossil.

Make a Guiness Book of Dinosaurs--largest, longest, heaviest, meanest, tallest, shortest, skinniest.

More Activities
Dinosaurs

Make a chart to show carnivores and herbivores. Define these terms and make a list of dinosaurs for each.

Make a web of careers that work with dinosaur fossils.

Make 10 Dinosaur Trivia cards.

Make a dinosaur crossword puzzle.

Write and recite a 4 stanza poem about dinosaurs.

Design a dinosaur mobile— that looks like a dinosaur.

Make a dinosaur skeleton. Use popsicle sticks, cardboard, toothpicks, and glue.

Construct a dinosaur game with a dinosaur-shaped gameboard.

Make a comic book about finding a dinosaur fossil.

Make a mural to show what reptiles lived in the sea long ago.

Make a poster of the fiercest dinosaur. List 10 facts about it.

Create an advertisement for a product that rids your lawn of dinosaurs.

Portfolio Activity

Name _____

Date _____ **Thematic Unit** _____

Activity _____

_____

_____

Objective _____

Learning Style(s) _____

Product(s) _____

Assessment Criteria	1	2	3	4	5
Organization					
Clarity of thought					
Process follow-through					
Grammar					
Thoroughness					
Resources					
Time Management					
Understanding					
Creativity					
Quality of Presentation					

_____

_____

_____

_____

_____

Content Areas
☐ Math ☐ English ☐ Reading ☐ Art ☐ Social Studies ☐ Science
☐ Music ☐ _____

Famous People

Create a T shirt showing your famous person and tell about the person on the back of the shirt.

What would happen if George Washington met Bill Clinton? What would Washington ask Clinton?

Color a limited edition paper plate honoring a famous person.

Draw a coat of arms for an important person. Include writing and pictures to describe your person.

Assemble a collage showing women in different occupations.

Make a bag puppet of a famous scientist. Write a script for the puppet. Have the puppet "tell" about his or her life.

Design a postcard about a person in military history.

Make an information cube about a famous explorer.

Read a play by Shakespeare. Tell the plot using 90's vocabulary and appropriate slang.

Write a conversation between Susan B. Anthony and Rush Limbaugh.

Listen to the evening news. Record the names in the news. Graph how many are famous, infamous, and unknown. Graph how many are men, women, and children.

List the top 10 characteristics of a hero. Then list 4 people who have those characteristics.

Choose a person you think showed courage. Construct an award for them. Write a speech to present the award.

Would you rather be a famous writer or a famous TV newscaster? Why?

Make a web of a famous musician. Include 12-15 facts and pictures.

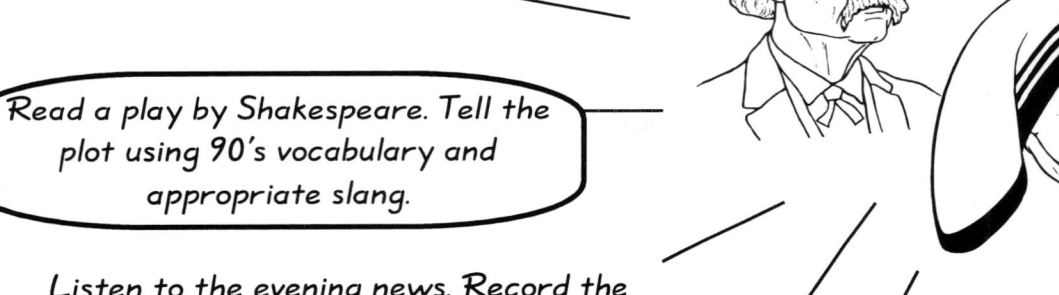

More Activities
Famous People

Choose 1 author. Make a book cover for his or her NEXT book.

List North American explorers and label their paths on a map.

Copy & memorize one of Robert Frost's poems. Illustrate it.

Give an oral report with visuals about a famous mathematician.

Make a "Women's Hall of Fame."

Select a signer of the Constitution and report about him in first person.

Choose 5 people who were important in human rights issues and write a paragraph about each one.

Construct a diorama of an important scene from history that includes a famous person.

Make a WHO AM I? riddle book. Include 5 people with at least 7 hints for each.

Make a collage of Sports Greats. On a separate piece of paper identify them and explain their sports and social achievements.

Choose an artist. Tell about his or her work. Illustrate a piece to show to the class.

Portfolio Activity

Name _____

Date _____ **Thematic Unit** _____

Activity _____

_____

_____

Objective _____

Learning Style(s) _____

Product(s) _____

Assessment Criteria	1	2	3	4	5
Organization					
Clarity of thought					
Process follow-through					
Grammar					
Thoroughness					
Resources					
Time Management					
Understanding					
Creativity					
Quality of Presentation					

_____

_____

_____

_____

Content Areas

☐ Math ☐ English ☐ Reading ☐ Art ☐ Social Studies ☐ Science
☐ Music ☐ _____

Flowers

Pretend you are an impatiens. Convince the aphids to stay away from you.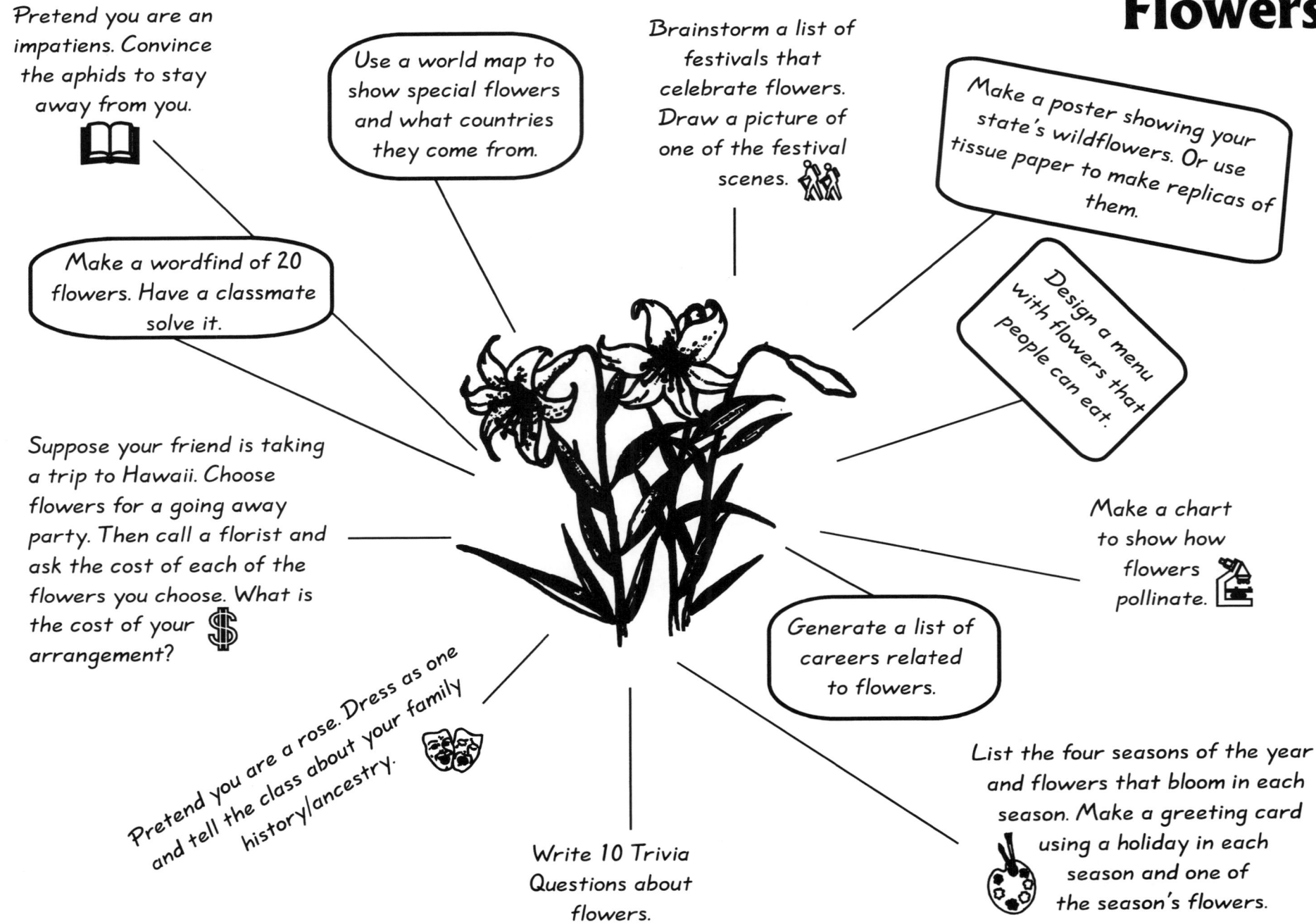

Use a world map to show special flowers and what countries they come from.

Brainstorm a list of festivals that celebrate flowers. Draw a picture of one of the festival scenes.

Make a poster showing your state's wildflowers. Or use tissue paper to make replicas of them.

Make a wordfind of 20 flowers. Have a classmate solve it.

Design a menu with flowers that people can eat.

Suppose your friend is taking a trip to Hawaii. Choose flowers for a going away party. Then call a florist and ask the cost of each of the flowers you choose. What is the cost of your arrangement?

Make a chart to show how flowers pollinate.

Generate a list of careers related to flowers.

Pretend you are a rose. Dress as one and tell the class about your family history/ancestry.

Write 10 Trivia Questions about flowers.

List the four seasons of the year and flowers that bloom in each season. Make a greeting card using a holiday in each season and one of the season's flowers.

More Activities
Flowers

Use magazines to make a scrapbook of flowers. Label them.

Design a mini-mural to show flowering plants used to make perfume.

Make a dictionary of flowering weeds.

Call florists to find the most expensive, most requested, and rarest kinds of flowers.

Design a poster to show the 50 states and their state flowers.

Invite a florist to class.

Design your own flower garden. Label the flowers.

Make a mini-poster illustrating prairie flowers.

Find out about the nasturtium. Illustrate.

Make a mini-book about night blooming flowers.

Design a mini-book about the tulip and its history.

Create a chart to show carnivorus plants.

Write a conversation between a flower's roots and its petals during a storm after a 4-week drought.

Design a fold-out of desert flowers. Tell one fact about each one and illustrate.

What are annuals, biennials, and perennials?

Portfolio Activity

Name _____

Date _____ **Thematic Unit** _____

Activity _____

_____

_____

Objective _____

Learning Style(s) _____

Product(s) _____

Assessment Criteria	1	2	3	4	5
Organization					
Clarity of thought					
Process follow-through					
Grammar					
Thoroughness					
Resources					
Time Management					
Understanding					
Creativity					
Quality of Presentation					

_____

_____

_____

_____

Content Areas

☐ Math ☐ English ☐ Reading ☐ Art ☐ Social Studies ☐ Science
☐ Music ☐ _____

Food for Thought

Plan a meal for a vegetarian. Bring samples to the class to taste test. Evaluate their tastiness.

Illustrate 5 kinds of garden scarecrows. Tell why they are good scarecrows.

Construct a hydroponic garden.

Take a survey to see who has worked in a garden. Make a graph to show your results.

Dress up as Thomas or Martha Jefferson. Explain how Thomas introduced potatoes and tomatoes.

Write a report about what good soil is and how to prepare soil for planting.

Design a chart to show and explain helpful and harmful insects in the garden. Write 5 facts you can deduce from the chart.

Use a US map to label places where we get our vegetables from in the winter.

Make a web of careers related to "gardening".

Create a mobile with at least 5 instructions about caring for your garden.

Design a poster that teaches how to use garden tools.

Make a chart to show plants that grow wild and plants that people grow in gardens.

What would happen if there were no green vegetables? Write your answer in an essay.

Write a conversation among a tomato plant, an aphid, and a water sprinkler.

Grow your own lima bean plant. Keep a chart of its daily growth. Write 5 facts you can deduce from the chart.

Plant your own indoor herb garden. Tell some medical and mythical herb cures.

More Activities
Food for Thought

Choose a vegetable and make a time line to show how it grows.

Make 10 Garden Trivia cards.

Design a poster of garden vegetables and show what part of the plant they come from.

Make a dictionary of garden vegetables.

Draw a picture of a pioneer's kitchen garden and label the plants.

What is compost?

Make a list of foods American Indians grew and what they used them for.

Make a wordfind of garden vegetables.

List songs about food.

Plan a garden for your backyard. Draw and label your plants.

Create a brochure of weeds you can eat.

Why is George Washington Carver important?

How are worms helpful to gardens?

Write a report about Luther Burbank.

Design a vegetable garden that you could grow in a window box.

Portfolio Activity

Name _____

Date _____ **Thematic Unit** _____

Activity _____

_____

_____

Objective _____

Learning Style(s) _____

Product(s) _____

Assessment Criteria	1	2	3	4	5
Organization					
Clarity of thought					
Process follow-through					
Grammar					
Thoroughness					
Resources					
Time Management					
Understanding					
Creativity					
Quality of Presentation					

_____

_____

_____

_____

Content Areas

☐ Math ☐ English ☐ Reading ☐ Art ☐ Social Studies ☐ Science
☐ Music ☐ _____

Jazz-Jazz-Jazz

Make a jazz crossword puzzle. Include boogie-woogie, Pine top Smith, ragtime, cutting contests, Jelly Roll Morton, spirituals, jubilees, jazz, swing, "sweet" jazz, minstrels, Louis Armstrong, blues, W.C. Handy, bebob, and Dizzy Gillespie.

Make a list of at least 10 great jazz pianists. Play their music for the class. (Play yourself or bring tapes/CDs)

Make a travel brochure for New Orleans describing historial jazz sites and contemporary establishments to visit.

Write a report about how jazz got its name. Include a time line of its history.

Draw a world map. Identify countries that produced famous jazz musicians. Compare the types of jazz they played. What can you conclude?

Use a page of jazz sheet music. Identify note values. Which note values occur most often? Use a different piece of music. Are the results the same?

How does a trumpet make sound? Why is it a different sound than a saxaphone?

Design a poster that tells about James Bland and minstrel shows. List minstrel songs, dances, and illustrate instruments.

Make a Jazz Mobile with 5 sections answering "Who, What, When, Where, Why."

Make a diorama of Congo Square in New Orleans. Tape record background jazz and play it as you tell why Congo Square is important.

Make an advertisement in print, video, or record for radio, information about the upcoming concert by the great "Swing Orchestras."

Compare / contrast "cool" or "progressive" jazz and "Dixieland" jazz. Write an essay explaining why you like one kind more than the other.

More Activities
Jazz-Jazz-Jazz

Make a poster that illustrates the serenade wagons in New Orleans.

Make a dictionary explaining the 10 basic elements of jazz.

Identify famous jazz musicians, their instruments, and where they are from.

What is "Improvising"? Besides in jazz, list places you can improvise.

What questions would a saxaphone in a marching band ask a saxaphone in a jazz band?

Make a list of types of "work" songs and tell why they were important to the making of Jazz.

Make a mobile showing the Jazz instruments.

Write a poem about the history of Jazz.

Make a crossword puzzle entitled "JAZZ".

Report about "oo-ya-koo" syllables and the famous people that sang them.

Make a map of the US and label the kinds of music you would find in different sections of the country 150 years ago.

Portfolio Activity

Name _____

Date _____ **Thematic Unit**

Activity _____

_____

_____

Objective _____

Learning Style(s) _____

Product(s) _____

Assessment Criteria	1	2	3	4	5
Organization					
Clarity of thought					
Process follow-through					
Grammar					
Thoroughness					
Resources					
Time Management					
Understanding					
Creativity					
Quality of Presentation					

_____

_____

_____

_____

Content Areas
☐ Math ☐ English ☐ Reading ☐ Art ☐ Social Studies ☐ Science
☐ Music ☐ _____

Government

Make a dictionary of government words that are important for a student to know. Make 7 ten-word sentences. Use one dictionary word in each sentence.

The Executive Branch has 12 departments. Make a calendar. For each month illustrate jobs in a branch.

Make a list of questions you would ask someone interviewing for a job in your prinipal's office.

Survey student's parents. Tabulate results and graph the jobs parents have in local government.

Make a poster showing the 3 main branches of government and list 6 different jobs for each one.

Do a report on the history of the White House.

What is the National Endowment for the Arts? Does your city or school benefit from it? How? Would you like to? How could you help?

$ If you were in charge of the school budget how much money would you give to the principal, teachers, sports teams, science classes, and gifted classes? Give reasons to support your decisions.

Make a cartoon strip about what you would do if you were president.

Draw a map of Washington D.C. and label some important buildings. Make a model of one of the monuments.

Make fact cards about the government. Create a game from the cards.

What science research does the government pay for? Give an example of some research that affects you.

State a law you would like passed in your town. What steps do you have to take to get it passed? Do them! Keep a journal of the process.

Design a travel brochure describing all the important places to visit in Washington D.C.

More Activities
Government

What are the qualifications to be President and Vice President? Who was the youngest and oldest President and Vice President? Is it better to have younger or older Presidents and Vice Presidents? Write your opinion in an essay.

Make a mobile to represent the 3 branches of government — and use branches!

Make 10 Government Trivia cards.

Make a crossword puzzle of jobs in your city government.

Compare / contrast the duties of the federal government, the state government, and the local government.

Attend a city council meeting. What part can you take in the meeting? What would happen if only people under 20 years of age could be on the council?

How is the Post Office different from other parts of government?

Name the political parties in the US. Draw their symbols. Compare / contrast them.

What do members of Congress DO? Write your Senator or House Representative. Ask for a schedule of a typical day.

"Shadow" a city official. Write a journal entry for your day.

Portfolio Activity

Name _____

Date _____ **Thematic Unit** _____

Activity _____

_____

_____

Objective _____

Learning Style(s) _____

Product(s) _____

Assessment Criteria	1	2	3	4	5
Organization					
Clarity of thought					
Process follow-through					
Grammar					
Thoroughness					
Resources					
Time Management					
Understanding					
Creativity					
Quality of Presentation					

_____

_____

_____

_____

Content Areas
☐ Math ☐ English ☐ Reading ☐ Art ☐ Social Studies ☐ Science
☐ Music ☐ _____

Literature Awareness

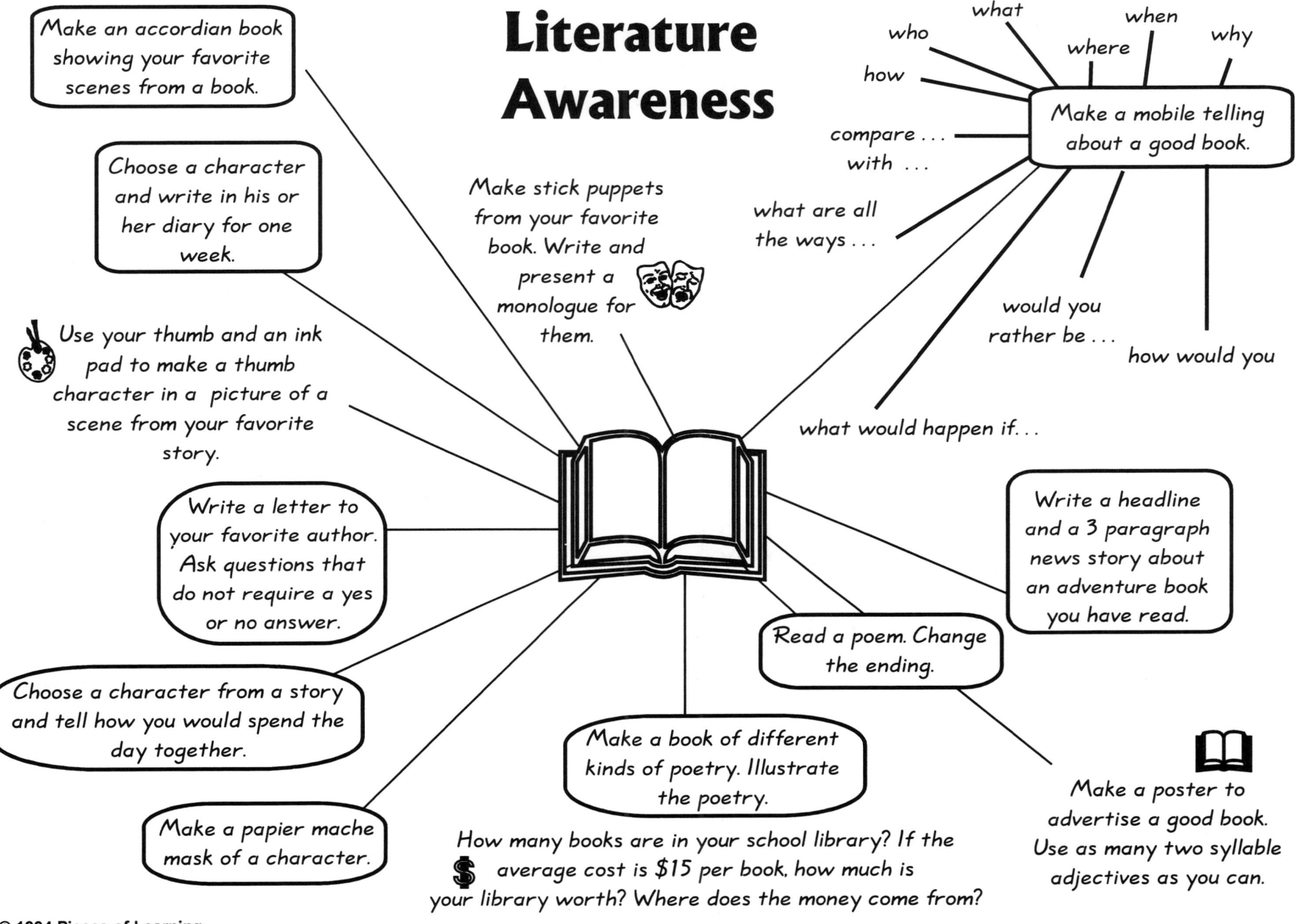

Make an accordian book showing your favorite scenes from a book.

Choose a character and write in his or her diary for one week.

Use your thumb and an ink pad to make a thumb character in a picture of a scene from your favorite story.

Make stick puppets from your favorite book. Write and present a monologue for them.

who what when why
how where
compare . . . with . . .
what are all the ways . . .
Make a mobile telling about a good book.
would you rather be . . .
how would you
what would happen if. . .

Write a letter to your favorite author. Ask questions that do not require a yes or no answer.

Choose a character from a story and tell how you would spend the day together.

Make a papier mache mask of a character.

Make a book of different kinds of poetry. Illustrate the poetry.

Read a poem. Change the ending.

Write a headline and a 3 paragraph news story about an adventure book you have read.

Make a poster to advertise a good book. Use as many two syllable adjectives as you can.

How many books are in your school library? If the average cost is $15 per book, how much is your library worth? Where does the money come from?

More Activities Literature

Make a diorama of the most important scene from your book. Explain why it is most important.

Draw a scene from your book. Then make a jigsaw puzzle from it.

Make a cover for your book.

Design a newspaper front page that tells you all about books.

Garfield and Charlie Brown are cartoon characters with their own books. Turn your book character into a cartoon strip.

Memorize 2 poems by the same author. Recite them dressed as the author.

Make a wordfind using at least 20 authors' names.

Make a crossword puzzle using Caldecott and Newbery Award winner titles.

Draw a time line of a book's plot.

Choose a story character. Add that character to the plot of a classmate's story. Together write a new story.

Role play your favorite book character.

Make a "Who's Who" of favorite book characters..

Make a mini-mural of your favorite poem.

Using a paper bag make the head of a memorable book chaacter.

Portfolio Activity

Name _____

Date _____ **Thematic Unit** _____

Activity _____

_____

_____

Objective _____

Learning Style(s) _____

Product(s) _____

Assessment Criteria	1	2	3	4	5
Organization					
Clarity of thought					
Process follow-through					
Grammar					
Thoroughness					
Resources					
Time Management					
Understanding					
Creativity					
Quality of Presentation					

_____

_____

_____

_____

Content Areas
☐ Math ☐ English ☐ Reading ☐ Art ☐ Social Studies ☐ Science
☐ Music ☐ _____

Fun with Math

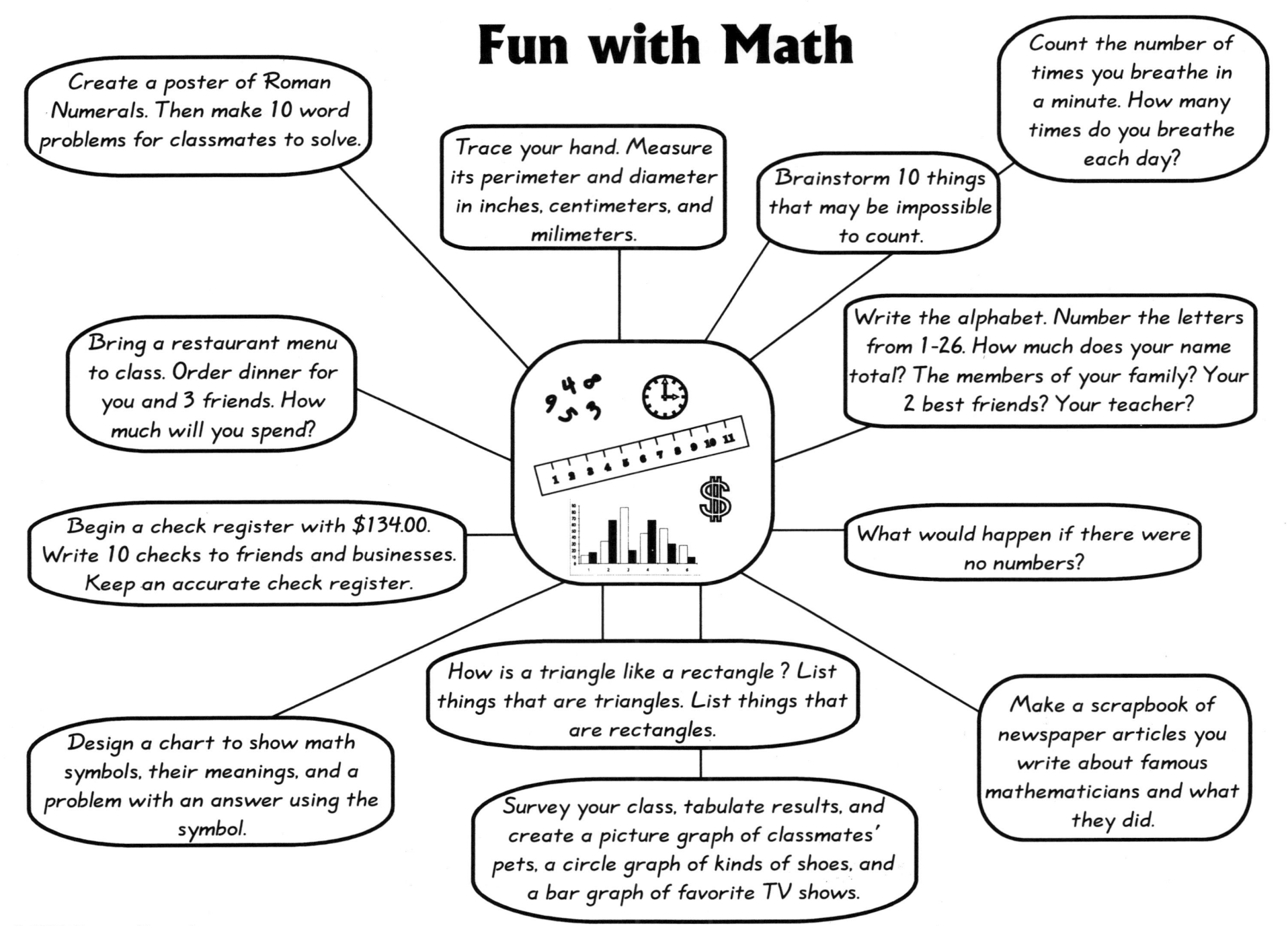

Create a poster of Roman Numerals. Then make 10 word problems for classmates to solve.

Trace your hand. Measure its perimeter and diameter in inches, centimeters, and milimeters.

Brainstorm 10 things that may be impossible to count.

Count the number of times you breathe in a minute. How many times do you breathe each day?

Bring a restaurant menu to class. Order dinner for you and 3 friends. How much will you spend?

Write the alphabet. Number the letters from 1-26. How much does your name total? The members of your family? Your 2 best friends? Your teacher?

Begin a check register with $134.00. Write 10 checks to friends and businesses. Keep an accurate check register.

What would happen if there were no numbers?

Design a chart to show math symbols, their meanings, and a problem with an answer using the symbol.

How is a triangle like a rectangle? List things that are triangles. List things that are rectangles.

Make a scrapbook of newspaper articles you write about famous mathematicians and what they did.

Survey your class, tabulate results, and create a picture graph of classmates' pets, a circle graph of kinds of shoes, and a bar graph of favorite TV shows.

More Activities
Fun with Math

Use cubes to make your initials. Find the perimeter of each of the letters. Do the same with a friend's intials.

Use the telephone book to list the area codes in your state. Then list them in order from smallest to largest. Make up 5 word problems with these numbers.

Measure 4 parts of your body and list them in order from shortest to longest.

Draw a picture using only the multiplication facts.

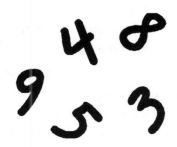

Design a math game and then play it with friends.

Make a chart of 19 shapes. Then list the name of an object for each geometric shape.

Make a list of weight measurements and list things that each could measure.

Find 1 of something in your classroom. Then 2, then 3 and so on. See how many numbers of something you can find. Illustrate your findings.

Invent a rap to learn about fractions.

List things that can be divided evenly. List things that cannot be divided.

Create a poster of big numbers (start with one million) and list something that might be counted with each big number.

Portfolio Activity

Name _____

Date _____ **Thematic Unit** _____

Activity _____

_____

_____

_____

Objective _____

Learning Style(s) _____

Product(s) _____

Assessment Criteria	1	2	3	4	5
Organization					
Clarity of thought					
Process follow-through					
Grammar					
Thoroughness					
Resources					
Time Management					
Understanding					
Creativity					
Quality of Presentation					

_____

_____

_____

_____

Content Areas

☐ Math ☐ English ☐ Reading ☐ Art ☐ Social Studies ☐ Science
☐ Music ☐ _____

Matter & Energy

Form a group. Assign each student to be a particular atom. Identify yourself with a piece of paper taped to your back. Form different simple molecules from student atoms.

What is an echo? And why is it important in a theater? Where else is it important? Why?

Make a web of different kinds of engines and indicate what they power.

Would you rather be an inventor of machines or the person who sells them? Why?

What would happen if there were no hydrogen?

Make a wind chime. Write a haiku about the sounds it makes.

What would happen if cold air could rise and hot air would sink?

Besides the Theory of Relativity, what is Albert Einstein famous for?

Design a brochure to show how sound travels and how fast it travels.

Using H, O, N, C atoms list all the different molecules you could make.

Write a report about the kite and how Ben Franklin used it for experiments. How does that experiment affect our daily lives?

Why are planes built in different shapes? Draw 2 differently shaped planes and tell what jobs they do.

Make a magazine picture collage of different types of matter.

Build different molecules using toothpicks and small marshmallows.

More Activities
Matter & Energy

What happens when something is heated? How does heat travel? How does hot air rise?

How does a pressure cooker work?

Make a lever and show how it works.

Write a report on light and how it travels.

Make a mini-book to show how electricity is made, distributed, and used.

Show how a magnet works.

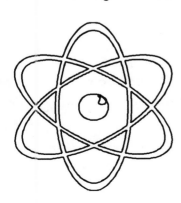

Make a brochure of different kinds of energy and their student uses.

Show the class how a pulley works. Name jobs that require pulleys.

Show how the same thing can have more than one state of matter.

Write a dialog between a flame and air above it.

Would you rather have a gas-driven or electricity-driven car? Why?

Make 10 Matter & Energy Trivia cards.

Explain static electricity. Make a time line to tell about Dinesh Bahadur, the master kiteman.

Portfolio Activity

Name _____

Date _____ **Thematic Unit** _____

Activity _____

_____

_____

Objective _____

Learning Style(s) _____

Product(s) _____

Assessment Criteria	1	2	3	4	5
Organization					
Clarity of thought					
Process follow-through					
Grammar					
Thoroughness					
Resources					
Time Management					
Understanding					
Creativity					
Quality of Presentation					

_____

_____

_____

_____

_____

Content Areas

☐ Math ☐ English ☐ Reading ☐ Art ☐ Social Studies ☐ Science
☐ Music ☐ _____

The Orient Connection

Write descriptions comparing / contrasting North Korea, South Korea, Taiwan, Japan, and China. Include cultural differences. What conclusions can you make about the Orient?

How are the governments of the Orient similar to ours?

Make a time line of discoveries and inventions from the Orient. Illustrate several on the time line. Which are most important to us today? Why?

Make a list of animals that make their homes in the Orient. Are any animals different from animals in our country? Find pictures of them or illustrate them. Why is the Orient a good place for them to live?

Make a model of a temple from the Far East. List activities that take place there. Name religions that have temples.

Make a web of sports played in China. How are they different from US sports?

Make a chart of 3 Oriental countries. List 3 things that each country exports to the US. What conclusions can you draw from this information?

Construct an abacus. Tell how it works. Compare / contrast it with American math.

Design a cookbook of Oriental food. Serve samples to the class. Tell where each originates.

Write a dialogue between a National Geographic interviewer and an ambassador from the Far East. Ask information about Mt. Fuji, water buffalo, silk, rice, and the Great China Wall.

Write a haiku about Confucious.

Demonstrate origami.

More Activities
Orient Connection

Investigate Japanese trains. Tell about their history. How are they different from trains in the US?

Design a travel brochure of an Oriental country.

Why did Christopher Columbus want to find a better route to the Far East?

Compare and contrast the schools in the Oriental countries. Then compare and contrast them with American schools; English schools; German schools.

What is the connection between Hong Kong and England?

Describe the conflict between North and South Korea. Conduct a survey to determine if adults agree or disagree with the ideas of either North or South Korea and why.

What would happen if North Korea, the United States, and Iraq were the only countries with nuclear weapons?

Report on Nagano, Japan, the site of the 1998 Olympics. Create a new event to enter into competition.

Portfolio Activity

Name

Date   **Thematic Unit**

Activity

_____

_____

_____

Objective

Learning Style(s)

Product(s)

Assessment Criteria	1	2	3	4	5
Organization					
Clarity of thought					
Process follow-through					
Grammar					
Thoroughness					
Resources					
Time Management					
Understanding					
Creativity					
Quality of Presentation					

Content Areas
☐ Math ☐ English ☐ Reading ☐ Art ☐ Social Studies ☐ Science
☐ Music ☐ _____

Plants and Trees

Research algae--seaweed, kelp, gulfweed, dulse, rockweed, and sea lettuce. Make some from crepe paper.

Design mini-murals showing plants that live in your city; in jungles; in deserts.

Make a scrapbook of carnivorous plants. Use definitions and pictures.

Choose a tree in your neighborhood. Write a story entitled "The Community of Maple" (or whatever tree you choose.) Tell about all the community members and what happens on a typical day in each of the four seasons of the year.

Design a wordfind of all the careers people have because of plants or trees. Write a cinquain using one of the words.

Draw a mural showing some plant communities in a northern forest and a southern desert.

Contact the county extension office. Borrow a soil testing kit. Test samples of dirt from different places (home, school, park).

Survey a 5 square block area. How many trees are in each block? What is the average number of trees per block? Why are trees necessary in land development? Make a scale model of the 5 square blocks.

What if only red plants could make food?

Pantomime how some seeds travel.

Write a report on soil bacteria and how it helps plants. Show bacteria under a microscope.

More Activities
Plants & Trees

Create a mini-book to show how bees help flowers.

Make a list of some fruits of plants that people eat.

Illustrate the differences among lichens, mosses, and ferns.

Write a report on roots and make a list of the ones people eat.

Explain why only green plants can make food.

Write a plant poem.

Draw and label a fold-out explaining photosynthesis.

Choose a plant and draw a time line of its growth.

Make a dictionary of plant words you have learned.

What would happen if all trees were evergreen trees?

Would you rather have no plants or no trees? Why? What effect would it have on human life?

List all the ways plants help man. Then list all the ways man helps plants.

Design a magazine that tells you facts about fungi.

Make 10 Plant Trivia cards.

Find out how deciduous trees live during the cold winter months.

Portfolio Activity

Name _____

Date _____ **Thematic Unit** _____

Activity _____

_____

_____

Objective _____

Learning Style(s) _____

Product(s) _____

Assessment Criteria	1	2	3	4	5
Organization					
Clarity of thought					
Process follow-through					
Grammar					
Thoroughness					
Resources					
Time Management					
Understanding					
Creativity					
Quality of Presentation					

_____

_____

_____

_____

Content Areas

☐ Math ☐ English ☐ Reading ☐ Art ☐ Social Studies ☐ Science
☐ Music ☐ _____

Theater

Brainstorm a list of the top 10 actors and actresses in the theater. Identify their current or last roles, play titles and year(s) they played.

Make a list of your city's or region's theaters - old and new. Tell about the history of one.

Survey, tabulate, and graph results of classmates who have been to a theater play.

Why is "The Phantom of the Opera" so popular with all age groups? Write your opinion in an essay.

Perform some of the sound effects that are made in the theater. Investigate acoustics and their importance in a theater.

Read about vaudeville. Perform a vaudeville act with a partner. Answer questions from the audience about vaudeville after your act.

Pick a current Broadway show. Why is it chosen to be on Broadway? Tell its theme in a poem.

Make a model of a set. Record an information tape telling about the stage, set, and props.

Make a model of Shakespeare's Globe Theater. Identify areas. List 5 interesting facts in a brochure.

Make a compare / contrast chart about opera, operetta, and comedic opera. List examples of each. Write 5 facts you can deduce from the chart.

Imagine you are a costume designer. In a costume you have designed tell the class about your job and who you have designed costumes for.

Create a time line showing how a theater gets ready for a performance.

More Activities
Theater

Design an illustrated Theater Dictionary.

What is "theater in the round"? Make a model of one. Explain its history.

What is the history of the saying "Break a Leg"? List other theatrical sayings, what they mean, and their origin.

Investigate the Tony Awards. List theatricals that have won the Award for the past 3 years. Have any been made into movies? If so, show one to the class. Would you rather be a prop or a set? Why?

Research famous theaters. Show pictures to the class or illustrate on a mini-mural. Identify their locations.

How is theater like a book? How is it different?

You are a theater critic. List criteria for evaluating a play. Exchange your list with another student. Defend your criteria.

Brainstorm jobs of a stage-hand. What famous actors and actresses and comedians were once stage hands?

Make a web of all the careers associated with the theater. Indicate by color which take a college education, high school education, special schools.

Why is theater important in our lives? List 5 reasons.

Portfolio Activity

Name _____

Date _____ **Thematic Unit** _____

Activity _____

_____

_____

Objective _____

Learning Style(s) _____

Product(s) _____

Assessment Criteria	1	2	3	4	5
Organization					
Clarity of thought					
Process follow-through					
Grammar					
Thoroughness					
Resources					
Time Management					
Understanding					
Creativity					
Quality of Presentation					

_____

_____

_____

_____

_____

Content Areas
☐ Math ☐ English ☐ Reading ☐ Art ☐ Social Studies ☐ Science
☐ Music ☐ _____

Trails from the Past

Make a totem pole that represents your family. Explain its significance.

Research an early American inventor. Include a picture or illustration of the invention(s).

Make a wanted poster of a famous outlaw. Compare & contrast personality traits of the sheriff and the outlaw.

Write a news article about a founder of your state. Tell about his/her ancestors living today.

Construct a diorama of a settler village or a ranch.

Make a poster of 6 traditional Native American shelters.

Which was more important - the Oregon Trail or the path to the moon by the astronauts? Give 3 reasons.

Use a map to locate and label the 26 states that have Native American names.

How did settlers make soap? Demonstrate.

Investigate the weather probably encountered by a wagon train traveling from Independence MO on the Santa Fe or Oregon Trail. Keep a Weather Journal of the trip.

Draw a cowboy in full costume and label the apparel. Tell the usefulness of each piece.

Design a coloring book of early American fashion.

Make a chart comparing children's chores in early America with yours today. Illustrate 1 of each.

Write a report describing how settlers made dipped candles. Try at home and bring your results to class.

Make 10 fact cards about a Native American tribe that lived in your state.

Research & report on the history of the totem pole.

Create a cookbook of early American recipes. Explain why you use the chosen ingredients.

More Activities
Trails from the Past

Make a poster of Native American symbolic writing.

Research the Pony Express.

Research and report on the "Trail of Tears."

Research & make a poster of Native American art—textiles, basketry, beadwork, pottery, painting, skinwork.

Read a biography of a person who contributed to early American history and share it with the class.

Report on the Stetson hat and illustrate.

Make a list of 20 items found in a general store.

Research and report on the California Gold Rush.

Make a book of cowboy terms.

Write a paragraph about the history of branding and design a branding iron chart.

Look up autobiography and then write your own.

Make a time line of important dates in your state's history.

Find out how your state got its name.

Make a wordfind of games and activities that early Americans did for fun.

Research and report on early settlements in your state.

Portfolio Activity

Name _____

Date _____ **Thematic Unit** _____

Activity _____

_____

_____

Objective _____

Learning Style(s) _____

Product(s) _____

Assessment Criteria	1	2	3	4	5
Organization					
Clarity of thought					
Process follow-through					
Grammar					
Thoroughness					
Resources					
Time Management					
Understanding					
Creativity					
Quality of Presentation					

Content Areas
☐ Math ☐ English ☐ Reading ☐ Art ☐ Social Studies ☐ Science
☐ Music ☐ _____

Washington D.C. Then and Now

List the Education Budgets of the last 4 Administrations. What department has received the most money? Compare with the student population (48,000,000) the dollars per student. What conclusions can you make about each administration?

Write a journal entry for the first week for the first woman president. Write entries for her last week.

Research Jacqueline Kennedy. Explain her contributions when she was First Lady.

Sketch the Presidential Seal and explain it. Make a student seal and explain your symbols.

Make a poster showing coins and paper money that have presidents on them. Why were these presidents chosen?

Compare and contrast Martha Washington and Martha Jefferson.

Make a mini-book of "Did You Know" facts about the White House.

Illustrate a time line of modern conveniences that have been added to the White House.

Make a web of White House workers and their jobs. Compare the number of workers and their duties in 1950 and 1990. What consulsions can you make?

Make a "Who's Who" list of children that lived in the White House. Where are they now? What are they doing?

 Locate and label on a map the birthplace of each president. What conclusions can you make? Predict where the next 4 presidents will come from.

Make a collage by illustrating or cutting from magazines pets of the White House. LIst names, dates, and owners.

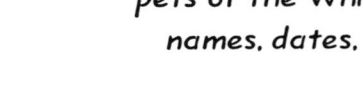 Video or tape record for TV or radio "Where Have They Gone?" a show about the last 5 presidential LOSERS.

More Activities
Washington D.C.

Report on Abigal Adams and 3 other First Ladies of the 19th Century.

Make a scale floor plan of the White House. Label the rooms. How would you change the arrangement? Why?

Report on the presidents sculpted on Mt. Rushmore. Who would you have chosen? Why?

What would happen if the capital of the US was your town? List all the advantages and disadvantages.

Make a poster of "White House Firsts" with illustrations.

Design a Presidential or Congressional Trivia game.

Make a list of nicknames of presidents. Choose three. How did they get those nicknames?

Draw a picture of Benjamin Banneker and list 5 facts about him.

Suppose you are newly elected to Congress. What would you try to do during your term? Why?

Compose a song about Washington D.C. using the melody to "My Kind of Town."

Portfolio Activity

Name _____ **Thematic Unit** _____

Activity _____

_____

_____

_____

Learning Style(s) _____

Product(s) _____

Assessment Criteria	1	2	3	4	5
Organization					
Clarity of thought					
Process follow-through					
Grammar					
Thoroughness					
Resources					
Time Management					
Understanding					
Creativity					
Quality of Presentation					

_____

_____

_____

_____

Content Areas
☐ Math ☐ English ☐ Reading ☐ Art ☐ Social Studies ☐ Science
☐ Music ☐ _____

Water

Read about crustaceans. Tell how and where they live in an oral or written report with illustrations.

Would you rather be a bucket of water in Ethiopia or Switzerland? Why?

How do we make ocean water, river water, and polluted water drinkable?

Watch a video or filmstrip about water. Make an oral report with visuals to the class.

What would happen if there were no salt water? Write an essay describing the consequences.

Design a shark bookmark. List at least 5 facts.

Build a diorama of a pond. Include pond plants, fish, frogs, and insects.

Which is more important - hot or cold water? Why?

Illustrate an ocean food chain.

Construct an underwater city of the future. Label and explain its features.

Locate bodies of water in your city and state on a map. Label. Identify their uses.

Who is Eugenie Clark? Why is she famous? With a partner role play an interview with her.

Predict how long it will take a 1" ice cube to melt at 68 degrees F. Then try it!

Describe and illustrate icebergs.

Investigate the "Flood of '93." How does the flooding of the Mississippi River in 1993 still affect us?

Brainstorm 20 uses for water.

Make a mobile of freshwater fish using an umbrella as the mobile.

More Activities
Water

Make a book about ocean careers. Illustrate.

Read a non-fiction book about water or water life and do a science book report.

Choose a North American river. Use an atlas to find the location of the river. Then draw it on a map. Show how the river flows. Draw tributaries. Why is this river important?

Draw a diagram showing the water cycle and how it affects insects.

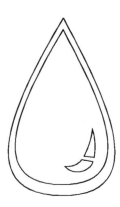

Make a poster illustrating 10 different shells.

Report on Jacques Cousteau.

Make an Ocean Trivia game.

Make a web of birds found near the ocean.

Make a dictionary of ocean words.

Draw a diagram of the ocean floor. Include the continental shelf and slope and basin.

Make a chart listing plants and animals under the headings "Fresh Water" and "Salt Water."

Illustrate the life cycle of a frog.

Categorize water animals as vertebrates and invertebrates. Illustrate two of each.

Portfolio Activity

Name _____

Date _____ Thematic Unit _____

Activity _____

_____

_____

Objective _____

Learning Style(s) _____

Product(s) _____

Assessment Criteria	1	2	3	4	5
Organization					
Clarity of thought					
Process follow-through					
Grammar					
Thoroughness					
Resources					
Time Management					
Understanding					
Creativity					
Quality of Presentation					

_____

_____

_____

_____

Content Areas
☐ Math ☐ English ☐ Reading ☐ Art ☐ Social Studies ☐ Science
☐ Music ☐ _____

Weather

Write a letter to a meteorologist to ask how he predicts the weather.

Make a mobile of weather instruments. Indicate what they measure. Explain how they measure. 9 4 8 5 3

Draw a picture of the possible destruction after a microburst.

Why does it rain? What things pollute the city air? How does weather affect our bodies? Explain how weather is important to farmers.

You are a square of sidewalk. Tell where you are located. Write 4 journal entries for January 1, April 15, June 16, and October 23.

Generate a list of all the songs you can find about weather. Write a "Singing Weather Forecast" for a radio or TV station. Video the forecast for TV.

How are snowflakes formed? Where does the white go when the snow melts?

Have an Australian fashion show. Wear and describe clothing for their 4 seasons during OUR four seasons.

Organize a debate between "winter" and "summer."

Make a weather station with model instruments.

Write a weather legend explaining why a particular kind of weather occurs today.

Predict how satellites forecast the weather. Then find out.

Make a web of the different kinds of storms. Use adjectives to describe them. Then tell when and where they occur and how they form.

© 1994 Pieces of Learning

More Activities
Weather

Investigate how tropical storms and hurricanes are named.

Explain how a volcano can affect the weather.

Make a Guiness Book of weather records.

Make a weather station. Draw a time line of how today's weather was forecasted for the past week. What can you conclude?

Make a scrapbook of weather poems.

Find out about Indian Rain Dances.

Call a college to find out what courses you have to take to be a meteorologist.

If you could change something about the climate where you live, what would it be? Why? What would the consequences be?

Is there really any difference between partly cloudy and partly sunny?

Make a list of jobs and careers that are affected by weather.

Take a survey. Make a graph. "What is the worst storm?"

Storytell weather myths.

Portfolio Activity

Name _____ **Thematic Unit** _____

Activity _____

_____

_____

_____

Learning Style(s) _____

Product(s) _____

Assessment Criteria   1   2   3   4   5

Organization

Clarity of thought

Process follow-through

Grammar

Thoroughness

Resources

Time Management

Understanding

Creativity

Quality of Presentation

_____

_____

_____

_____

Content Areas

☐ Math ☐ English ☐ Reading ☐ Art ☐ Social Studies ☐ Science
☐ Music ☐ _____

The Circus

List all the animals in a circus. What do they all have in common?

Create a wordfind of performing animals in the circus.

What was Buffalo Bill's Wild West Show? How was it different from the circus? How was it similar?

Have a panel discuss animal acts in the circus. Are they hurtful to animals?

Investigate clown make-up. Put it on in front of the class and explain its meaning.

How is Tom Thumb like Emmet Kelly?

Dress as a clown. Prepare a clown act. Pantomime to your classmates.

Survey classmates to find what circus jobs they would like. Make a graph to show the results.

On a world map indicate where famous circus acts come from.

Read about the circus in other countries. Make a compare/contrast chart. Write 5 facts you can deduce from the chart.

Read about circus acts. Design an advertisement for a newspaper announcing the circus coming to town.

Write for circus information and share with the class.

Circus Fans of America
c/o J. Allen
PO Box 69
Camp Hill PA 17011

Circus Historical Society
c/o Fred Pfening Jr.
2515 Dorset Road
Columbus OH 43221

Clown College
PO Box 1528
Venice FL 33595

More Activities
Circus

Describe how circus costumes are made. Then design one of your own.

Identify the history of the circus on a time line made of circus wagons.

Create a mini-book about Clown College. Include facts and clown faces.

List famous clowns. Compare /contrast their appearances and behaviors.

Create a large poster with 10 circus terms and pictures that explain them.

List Circus Headline acts of long ago.

Make a wordfind of circus jobs.

Write 10 Circus Trivia cards.

Make a model of the "Big Top" and fill it with circus acts.

How does someone get a Ringmaster's job? What questions would you ask in an interview for someone applying for the job?

Would you rather go to a circus or a comedy at the theater? Why?

What would happen if there were no entertainment?

Portfolio Activity

Name _____

Date _____ **Thematic Unit** _____

Activity _____

_____

_____

Objective _____

Learning Style(s) _____

Product(s) _____

Assessment Criteria	1	2	3	4	5
Organization					
Clarity of thought					
Process follow-through					
Grammar					
Thoroughness					
Resources					
Time Management					
Understanding					
Creativity					
Quality of Presentation					

_____

_____

_____

_____

_____

Content Areas

☐ Math ☐ English ☐ Reading ☐ Art ☐ Social Studies ☐ Science
☐ Music ☐ _____

We are Multi-cultural

Write a folktale about your city and the different people living there. 📖

List 7 famous scientists--one from each continent. What have they discovered or invented?

Generate a list of ethnic groups in your class. Invite parents to talk to the class about their ancestry and culture and the traditions they continue today.

Was your city or a city near you named after a famous person? Find out and write a story about why YOU think the city was named after him or her.

Make a web of all the ways you and a person from another culture are alike. Make a second web of all the ways you are different. What conclusions can you make from looking at the webs?

Write a poem about children from around the world.

Make a poster showing what people from other cultures think is "beautiful."

Take a survey of kids in the area to find out the types of "foreign" food they eat. Graph your results.

Make a world map and identify folktale titles in various countries. Share one of the tales with the class. Dress in costume.

Make a scrapbook of typical clothing of students from around the world.

Play games from 5 countries. Explain their history. How are they different from American games?

Design a magazine titled "Celebrations Around the World." Illustrate and tell about as many different kinds of celebrations as you can find.

More Activities
Multi-cultural

Illustrate a book of famous people from around the world. Identify why they are famous.

People from many cultures keep pets. On a blank world map draw pets that are popular in different countries.

Make a list of holidays from other countries. Then make an illustrated encyclopedia of the holidays.

Make a mural showing different kinds of hats from around the world. Identify the country they are from.

Make a wordfind of jobs important in other countries.

Read the poem "Harlem Sweeties" and make a list of all the skin colors.

Survey 10 students to find out where their ancestors are from. Label a world map to show your findings.

There are 201 different main languages spoken on earth. Why?

What would happen if no one understood another language besides their own?

Make a game about children's games around the world.

Portfolio Activity

Name _____

Date _____ **Thematic Unit** _____

Activity _____

_____

_____

Objective _____

Learning Style(s) _____

Product(s) _____

Assessment Criteria	1	2	3	4	5
Organization					
Clarity of thought					
Process follow-through					
Grammar					
Thoroughness					
Resources					
Time Management					
Understanding					
Creativity					
Quality of Presentation					

_____

_____

_____

_____

_____

Content Areas

☐ Math ☐ English ☐ Reading ☐ Art ☐ Social Studies ☐ Science
☐ Music ☐ _____

Rocks and Minerals

Why is coal a special rock? Describe ways it is mined and the consequences of types of mining.

Make a time line from discovery to locomotive - "The Life of Iron."

Some rocks form strange shapes. Draw 5 of them that are "famous" and identify their location.

On a US map locate where metals are found and mined. What conclusions can you make?

Make a mini-book of useful minerals. Illustrate and list at least 3 uses for each mineral.

Make a drawing illustrating 4 ways big rocks become small rocks.

Brainstorm a list of rocks and how people use them in their work.

Write a conversation between a metamorphic rock and an igneous rock on a hot summer's day.

Make a diorama of an open-pit mine.

On the computer make a wordfind of different types of sedimentary, metamorphic, and igenous rocks.

Would you rather be a diamond or a trilobite? Why? Would you rather own a diamond or a trilobite? Why?

Why are airplanes made of a large amount of titanium and aluminum?

What would have happened if the California Gold Rush of 1849 would have been ALL iron pyrite?

Make a word web of careers people have that deal with rocks or minerals.

Compare and contrast kinds of gems. Use categories such as value, location, color, use.

Write a poem about a fossil in a rock.

More Activities
Rocks & Minerals

Draw a time line to explain how machines get the metal out of ores.

Make a dictionary of the new "rock" words you have learned. Illustrate.

Make 10 Rocks and Minerals Trivia cards.

Design a mobile and show 7 ways scientists find out about rocks.

Draw a map of the United States and show where 6 different kinds of rocks OR 6 minerals are found.

Report on rocks in space.

Make a mini-poster to show the three minerals you can see in granite.

Often humans take vitamin pills that have minerals in them. How are the minerals in vitamin pills different from the minerals that are mined?

Would your rather be a miner or a gemologist? Why?

What is the significance of the Kimberley Great Hole?

What is the moon made of? How did it form?

How are fossils preserved in rocks?

Design a fold-out to show minerals shaped as crystals. Label your work.

Portfolio Activity

Name _____

Date _____ **Thematic Unit** _____

Activity _____

_____

_____

Objective _____

Learning Style(s) _____

Product(s) _____

Assessment Criteria	1	2	3	4	5
Organization					
Clarity of thought					
Process follow-through					
Grammar					
Thoroughness					
Resources					
Time Management					
Understanding					
Creativity					
Quality of Presentation					

_____

_____

_____

_____

_____

Content Areas

☐ Math ☐ English ☐ Reading ☐ Art ☐ Social Studies ☐ Science ☐ Music ☐ _____

Contemporary Social Studies

List alternatives to solve an American hostage crisis. As a group rank the best 5 solutions. Defend your rankings.

Suppose a group of German students was visiting your city during "Desert Storm." List 10 questions you expect them to ask and write the answers you would give.

Write a one-page essay either agreeing or disagreeing with the statement "The President should be given another 4 years in the White House because . . . ."

Write a recipe of 6 ingredients an American President should have. Explain your reasons for including each ingredient.

Select 10 song titles that describe US foreign policy in the 80s and 90s. Write 2-4 sentences explaining your reasons for including each song.

Choose 3 pictures from magazines that depict the 1990s. Make 4 inferences and 4 predictions about society from what you see.

You are the producer-director of a new television series. Name the show, tell what characters you would have each of the 20th Century American Presidents play on the show, and write 2-4 sentences giving your reasons for your role selections.

Field a baseball team with 20th Century American presidents. Which man would you assign to each position and why? Which 6 would you "sit the bench?" Why? Who would "pinch hit?" Why? Who would be a "relief pitcher?" Why?

More Activities Contemporary Social Studies

The following activities and the activities on the web were taken from the book **"Questioning Makes the Difference"** *by Nancy Johnson, Pieces of Learning ©1990, Roy Martin, originator.*

Pretend you are a newly elected president currently in the process of naming your cabinet. List characteristics that you feel are necessary for the posts of Secretary of State and Secretary of Defense. Who would you select from your class to fill the positions? Tell why you selected the people you did.

Prepare a front page for an American newspaper for December 7, 1941. Prepare another front page for a Japanese newspaper for the same day. Compare / contrast the newspapers.

Work with a partner (girl-boy). Suppose you are a 20th century President and the spouse. Carry on a conversation over lunch about the successes and failures of your presidency.

List 5 personality characteristics that you feel are the most important for a President of the United States to have. Then observe classmates and other students you know. Find someone who most closely fits your list. Discuss your experience choosing and observing with the class.

Portfolio Activity

Name _____

Date _____ **Thematic Unit** _____

Activity _____

_____

_____

Objective _____

Learning Style(s) _____

Product(s) _____

Assessment Criteria	1	2	3	4	5
Organization					
Clarity of thought					
Process follow-through					
Grammar					
Thoroughness					
Resources					
Time Management					
Understanding					
Creativity					
Quality of Presentation					

_____

_____

_____

_____

Content Areas

☐ Math ☐ English ☐ Reading ☐ Art ☐ Social Studies ☐ Science
☐ Music ☐ _____

Thingamajigs, Contraptions, Thingamabobs

Compare / contrast patents and copyrights as ways to protect an invention. Which have been most important? Why?

Create a Best-Friend Robot. Give your robot personal qualities. BE the robot and give a 2 minute TV commercial selling yourself.

Invent a game. Write instructions. Make the gameboard three-dimensional.

Choose your favorite "thingamajig" and describe how you would make it better, faster, smaller or bigger.

Make a crossword puzzle of Leonardo da Vinci's inventions.

Write a mini-book about Henry Ford's invention. Include your car of the future.

Make a contraption from paper. Explain how it works.

Write a letter to Thomas Edison thanking him for one of his inventions. Explain why it became so important after he died. Tell why it is important to you.

Use magazine pictures to create a collage of inventions in the 19th Century; in the 20th.

What is the difference between an invention and a discovery? Give examples.

Generate a list of the 10 inventions most important to you. What would you substitute for each of them if they were taken away from you? Persuade another student to accept your list as the "right" list.

Make a chart of safety inventions for senior citizens. Make copies of your chart and send them to "retirement villages." Ask residents to react to your choices and add some of their own.

Invent a hat that does something for you. Draw and label your invention. Or make it and wear it!

More Activities
Thingamajigs

Design a new cereal. Include a box. Tell what it does for you.

"Invent" a time line of famous inventions.

Cut out a full-sized person from butcher paper. Make him a famous inventor. Write all about him in the cut out.

Make a poster of "Stone Age Inventions."

Make up a quiz or trivia game about lazers.

Report on Leonardo da Vinci. Make a mobile of his inventions.

Design a kitchen of the future. Label the parts and what they do.

Construct a contraption.

Write about the school of the future.

Make a fashion book of future hats and shoes. Illustrate.

Portfolio Activity

Name _____

Date _____ **Thematic Unit** _____

Activity _____

_____

_____

Objective _____

Learning Style(s) _____

Product(s) _____

Assessment Criteria	1	2	3	4	5
Organization					
Clarity of thought					
Process follow-through					
Grammar					
Thoroughness					
Resources					
Time Management					
Understanding					
Creativity					
Quality of Presentation					

_____

_____

_____

_____

Content Areas
☐ Math ☐ English ☐ Reading ☐ Art ☐ Social Studies ☐ Science
☐ Music ☐ _____

The Tropical Rain Forest

Why is the rosy periwinkle an important rainforest flower?

What is the ecosystem of the rainforest? Design a food web to explain and describe it in a skit.

Make a rainforest job dictionary. What do rainforest specialists do? Why are they important? What job could they apply for if there were no more rainforests?

What other plants live in the rainforest besides bromeliads, stranglers, buttress root, lianas, and palms? Illustrate all of them.

What is your Senator's opinion about the destruction of the rainforests? Write a letter to him or her AND a follow-up letter to the response.

"The Great Kapok Tree" is a book dedicated to Chico Mendes. Who is he, why is he important, and why would this book be dedicated to him?

Make a compare / contrast chart of the Desert and the Rainforest. What 5 conclusions can you make?

What is bamboo and what is it used for? Illustrate a shoot and a field with workers in it.

What are the 4 layers of the rainforest? Illustrate them. Describe each. Which layer would you rather live in? Why?

Write a letter. What would a tree in the rainforest ask the president of a logging company?

List all the ways to save the rainforest. Give two supporting detail statements for each.

Make a web. What things do we get from the rainforest? If we could no longer get these things from the rainforest what could we substitute for them?

Read about the YANOMAMO - a tribe of Rainforest Indians. How do their lives compare with yours?

Why are rainforests called the "lungs" of the planet?

More Activities
The Rainforest

Explain epiphytes and make an illustrated list of them.

Design a poster to show the water cycle in the rainforest.

Make a list of reasons why people are destroying the rainforests.

What would happen if it stopped raining in the rainforest?

Draw a picture of a rainforest tree and tell how the shallow-rooted trees get their nourishment.

List of questions a cactus might ask a bamboo tree.

There are 4 kinds of rain-forests. Name them. Locate them on a world map. Compare/contrast their characteristics on a chart. In which rainforest would you rather live? Why?

You are a bird that lives in the rainforest. Who are you, what do you see, hear, and smell? What do you do?

Make a tape recording of sounds in the the rainforest.

Draw a snowforest; a desertforest; a flower-forest; or a monsterforest.

Decorate "The Bubble" as the rainforest and present products in "The Bubble."

Write a letter to
The Children's Rainforest
PO Box 936
Lewiston ME 04240

Portfolio Activity

Name _____

Date _____ **Thematic Unit** _____

Activity _____

_____

_____

Objective _____

Learning Style(s) _____

Product(s) _____

Assessment Criteria	1	2	3	4	5
Organization					
Clarity of thought					
Process follow-through					
Grammar					
Thoroughness					
Resources					
Time Management					
Understanding					
Creativity					
Quality of Presentation					

_____

_____

_____

_____

Content Areas
☐ Math ☐ English ☐ Reading ☐ Art ☐ Social Studies ☐ Science
☐ Music ☐ _____

Remembering

What are the "vapors"? Why would a lady swoon? Why would men duel? What is gamy language? To which category might all these words belong?

List home remedies for common illnesses that your grandparents had. Then list remedies used today. How do they compare to today's remedies?

Who was Kilroy?

Survey your grandparents. Find out what their first "kid" jobs were and how much they earned. Compare / contrast with the 1990s.

What 5 favorite things did people do in the evenings at home in the 1940s? the 1950s? How many do we still do? What has replaced some of them? Why?

Pedal pushers, bunting, hoopla, Burma Shave, scooters, Tom Mix, and Alf Landon are all good memories. Find out what they were. What things do you think you will remember 50 years from now? Which people? Why?

Compare / contrast roads and highways in the 1950s and today.

How is a grocery store, supermarket, or Superstore like the butcher shop of the 1920s? Would you rather buy things in the butcher shop or a modern store? Why? Where would your parents rather shop?

More Activities
Remembering

Do you remember the names of the Presidents who are sculpted on Mount Rushmore? Name them. Whose face was first sculpted to the LEFT of George Washington? Why is George Washington's face so far in front of the other faces?

What is milkweed floss? What was it used for by the Navy in World War II? What did it replace? Why did it have to be replaced?

Illustrate the following clothing or find these items and wear them to class: bobby socks, penny loafers, a fedora, a derby, bloomers, a poodle skirt and 'whoopee pants.' How did they get their names?

Where would you find a rumble seat? What was it used for?

What are each of the following kinds of apples used for: eaters, cookers, and leavings?

Interview your parents and grandparents. Ask them to describe games they played when they were young. Did they play "Annie Over" or "Duck, Duck, Goose?" Instruct your classmates how to play some of the games they played and play them with your classmates.

Portfolio Activity

Name _____

Date _____ **Thematic Unit**

Activity _____

_____

_____

Objective _____

Learning Style(s) _____

Product(s) _____

Assessment Criteria	1	2	3	4	5
Organization					
Clarity of thought					
Process follow-through					
Grammar					
Thoroughness					
Resources					
Time Management					
Understanding					
Creativity					
Quality of Presentation					

_____

_____

_____

_____

_____

Content Areas
☐ Math ☐ English ☐ Reading ☐ Art ☐ Social Studies ☐ Science
☐ Music ☐ _____

Where in the World?

What would happen if . . .
. . . huge deposits of minerals
were found here?
. . . the Olympics were held
here?
. . . nuclear weapons were
made here?
. . . oil was found here?

List all the countries that
. . . border this country
. . . import into
. . .are exported to from. . .
. . . speak the same language as. . .
. . . have the same currency as. . .

What questions would a student
from this country ask a US student;
What questions would you ask a
student from that country?

Make a History Mobile
Who
What
When
Where
Why
How

Compare and contrast with the United
States any of the following. Use a unique
visual to present your findings.
economy
topography
traditions
climate
government
agriculture
industry
schooling

Would you rather live in the north or south,
east or west? Give advantages and
disadvantages of living in each area.

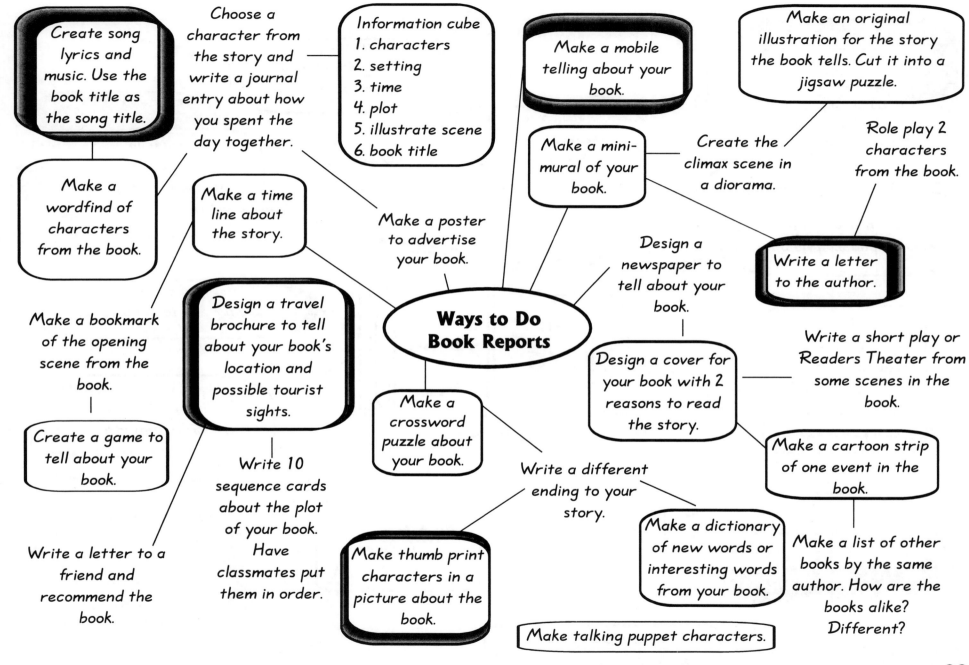

Create song lyrics and music. Use the book title as the song title.

Choose a character from the story and write a journal entry about how you spent the day together.

Information cube
1. characters
2. setting
3. time
4. plot
5. illustrate scene
6. book title

Make a mobile telling about your book.

Make an original illustration for the story the book tells. Cut it into a jigsaw puzzle.

Make a wordfind of characters from the book.

Make a time line about the story.

Make a mini-mural of your book.

Create the climax scene in a diorama.

Role play 2 characters from the book.

Make a poster to advertise your book.

Design a newspaper to tell about your book.

Write a letter to the author.

Make a bookmark of the opening scene from the book.

Design a travel brochure to tell about your book's location and possible tourist sights.

Ways to Do Book Reports

Write a short play or Readers Theater from some scenes in the book.

Create a game to tell about your book.

Make a crossword puzzle about your book.

Design a cover for your book with 2 reasons to read the story.

Make a cartoon strip of one event in the book.

Write a letter to a friend and recommend the book.

Write 10 sequence cards about the plot of your book. Have classmates put them in order.

Make thumb print characters in a picture about the book.

Write a different ending to your story.

Make a dictionary of new words or interesting words from your book.

Make a list of other books by the same author. How are the books alike? Different?

Make talking puppet characters.

99

Design a t-shirt to save your favorite tree.

Write a letter to the author's widow to tell her why you think the book is important.

Write a different ending for the story. Act it out.

Who speaks for our trees?

Write a poem about a neat tree.

Write a speech to tell people how important trees are. Give your speech to another class or the city council.

Generate a list of the ways the ONCE-LER polluted.

The Lorax **by Dr. Seuss**

Write a letter to your parents and convince them that all you want for your birthday is a tree to plant.

Draw a picture and describe the ecosystem of a Truffala Tree.

Find out about palm trees. Illustrate several and cite their differences.

Make a poster of a real tree and list 5 facts about it.

Make an advertisement for saving an interesting kind of a tree.

Make a list of things you could do with the Truffala Trees and not cut them down.

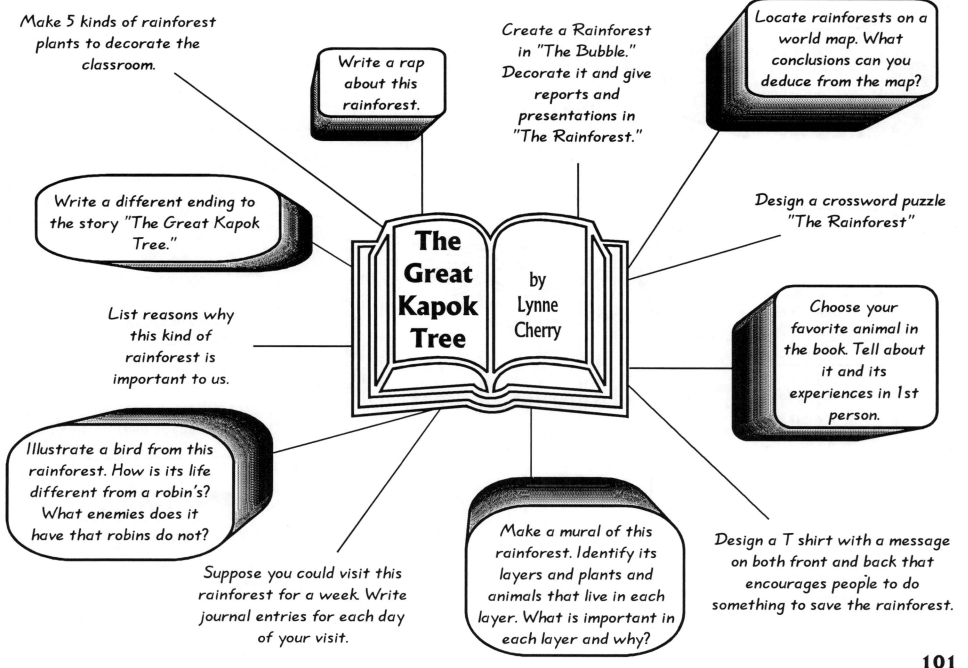

Make 5 kinds of rainforest plants to decorate the classroom.

Write a rap about this rainforest.

Create a Rainforest in "The Bubble." Decorate it and give reports and presentations in "The Rainforest."

Locate rainforests on a world map. What conclusions can you deduce from the map?

Write a different ending to the story "The Great Kapok Tree."

Design a crossword puzzle "The Rainforest"

The Great Kapok Tree by Lynne Cherry

List reasons why this kind of rainforest is important to us.

Choose your favorite animal in the book. Tell about it and its experiences in 1st person.

Illustrate a bird from this rainforest. How is its life different from a robin's? What enemies does it have that robins do not?

Suppose you could visit this rainforest for a week. Write journal entries for each day of your visit.

Make a mural of this rainforest. Identify its layers and plants and animals that live in each layer. What is important in each layer and why?

Design a T shirt with a message on both front and back that encourages people to do something to save the rainforest.

Make a list of other names for the Baobab. What are the reasons you would use the new names?

Make a puppet of one of the African birds that come to the Baobab tree. Write dialog to tell the class about it.

What fruit of the Baobab do the animals eat? Which animals eat it?

Draw a picture of the Baobab tree in its ecosystem.

Why are the Baobab flowers important?

Design a time line on a cut out of a tree to show the life of the Baobab.

Make a mural or collage to illustrate how the African people use the Baobab Tree.

Tree of Life

The World of the African Baobab

by Barbara Bash

Write a poem about the Baobab.

Write a report about why the branches of the Baobab tree look like gnarled roots. Then write a legend "How the Baobab Got Its Roots."

Write a letter to the author to tell her what you learned from her book and why it is important to you.

What is a savannah? Where are they located? Label them on a world map. Why are they important? To whom?

Draw a picture of the Baobab. List 5 facts about it. Predict what will happen to it in the year 2050. Why do you think this will happen?

Suppose you visited the Baobab. Write your experience as a journal.

Draw a picture of the Saguaro Cactus flower. Label its parts. Tell the animals that help pollinate it so it produces fruit.

Illustrate the ecosystem of the Saguaro Cactus. Compare / contrast to the ecosystem of a rainforest.

Make a clay map of North America. Identify with clay where the Giant Saguaro grows.

What are "saguaro boots" and how do the Indians use them?

Role play the Tohono O'odham Indians to show how they get and use the fruit of the Saguaro Cactus.

Draw a picture of the cactus and explain the use of the pleats and spines.

Desert Giant -
by
Barbara Bash
The World of the Saguaro Cactus

Write a poem about the Saguaro Cactus.

Make a wordfind of the animals that eat the fruit - then choose one and write a report about that animal.

Brainstorm reasons why the Saguaro Cactus is important. Include who, what, when, where in your reasons.

Write a letter to the author. Ask how she researched the information for the book. Tell her what you liked about the way she wrote the book.

Design a poster to show all the creatures that use the dead Saguaro Cactus.

On a cut out of a cactus make a time line of the life of a Saguaro Cactus.

103

Make a list of new words you learned in spelling this year and illustrate them.

Make a mini-book of your favorite story the teacher read. Be sure to use pictures.

Make a poster advertising your school as "The Best."

Make a time line of the events at school this year.

Choose your favorite web that you did this year and make a list of what you learned.

Write a "thank you" letter to your teacher or your parents.

Design a Progress Report for your teacher and fill it out!

Make a list of your friends at school and put them in ABC order.

Create a seek-and-find using names from people in the class.

Make a web showing all the thematic activities you did or questions you answered this year.

Make a list of the books you read this year. Recommend a book next year's class should read and tell why.

End of Year Web

Make the front page of a newspaper telling all the important events that happened in your class this year.

Draw a cartoon of one day in your life at school.

Draw a map of the school and label it using a legend.

Make a poster or mini-book about what you learned in class this year.

Make a list of the things you would change in class and how you would change them.

Write a story about the funniest thing that happened this year in school.

Create a poem about your year in school.

Make a flip chart of all the kinds of math problems you did this year.

Draw a picture that tells about your favorite computer program.

Activities

Duplicate this page. Cut on the dotted lines. Laminate the cards on heavy tagboard or index cards. Have students choose activities from the "stack" during unit work.

	Design a mobile with at least 6 facts	Write a letter for collecting information	Make a list of careers that exist	Draw and label a map	Make a list of books about your subject	Design a collage
Construct a game with at least 10 facts	Make a cartoon strip to tell some facts	Write a report and draw a picture	Draw and color a mini-mural Label the facts	Make a dictionary with pictures and definitions	Make a flipbook	Design a mini-book
Create a book cover to tell about your subject	Write a poem and illustrate it	Take a survey and make a graph	Make a model of plaster, clay, wood, or soap	Design a magazine with facts and pictures	Make up a quiz with 10 questions and answers	Make 10 Trivia cards
Make a chart to show similarities or differences	Make a scrapbook	Design a travel brochure	Make a wordfind	Create a montage	Draw a time line	Make a crossword puzzle
Write your own song—or find songs about your subject	Design a newspaper front page to give some facts	Design a bookmark with 3 facts	Make a fold-out chart of new words or expressions	Construct a diorama. Include 6 facts on an index card	Make a poster that teaches one or more facts	Make a television & a scroll story with facts and pictures

Journal Entries

_____

Portfolio Activity

Name _____

Date _____ **Thematic Unit** _____

Activity _____

_____

_____

Objective _____

Learning Style(s) _____

Product(s) _____

Assessment Criteria	1	2	3	4	5
Organization					
Clarity of thought					
Process follow-through					
Grammar					
Thoroughness					
Resources					
Time Management					
Understanding					
Creativity					
Quality of Presentation					

_____

_____

_____

_____

Content Areas

☐ Math ☐ English ☐ Reading ☐ Art ☐ Social Studies ☐ Science
☐ Music ☐ _____

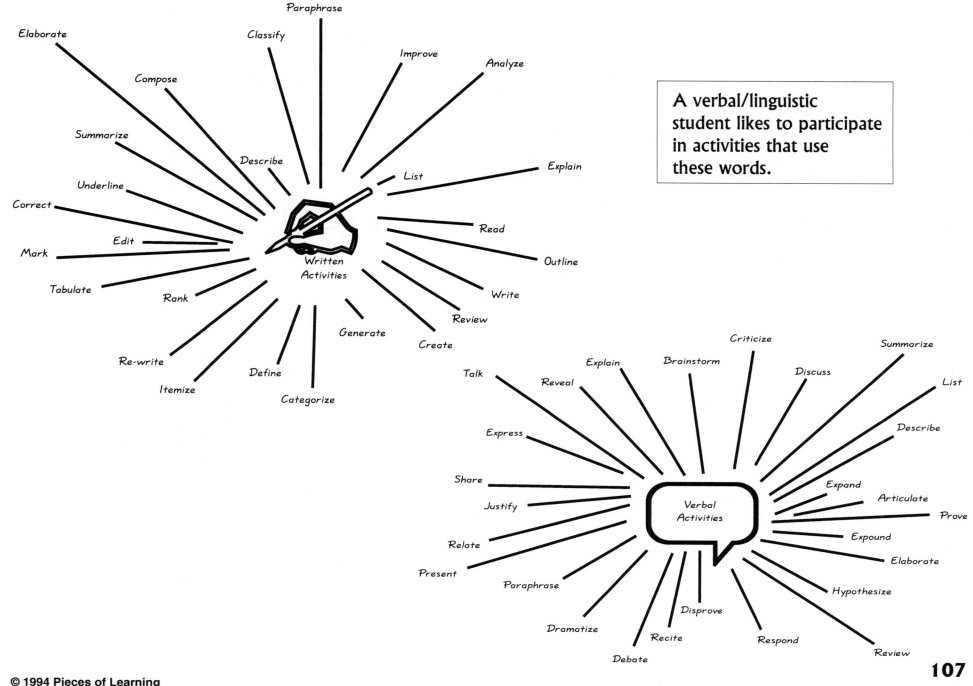

A verbal/linguistic student likes to participate in activities that use these words.

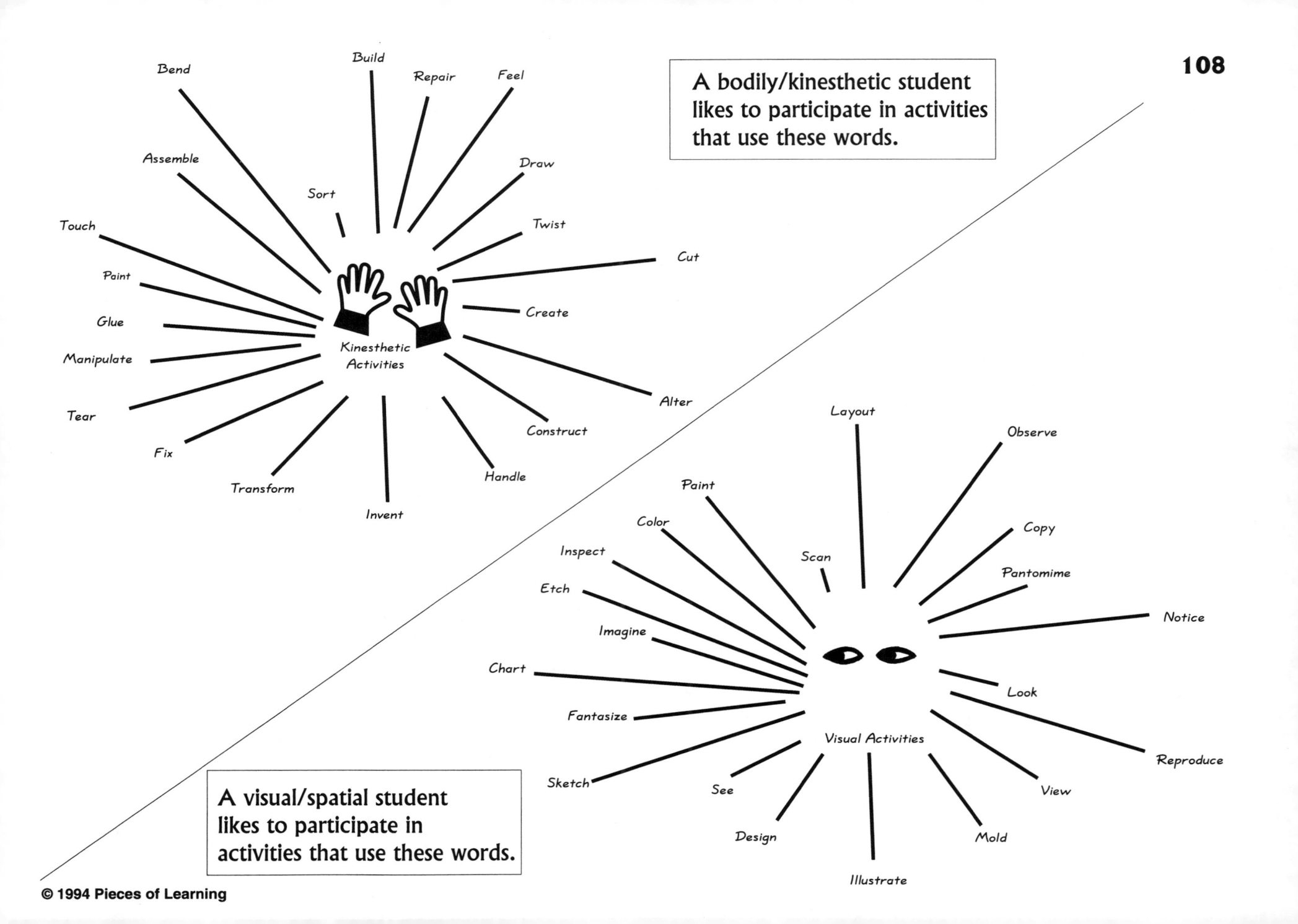

A bodily/kinesthetic student likes to participate in activities that use these words.

Bend
Build
Repair
Feel
Assemble
Draw
Sort
Twist
Touch
Cut
Paint
Create
Glue
Kinesthetic Activities
Manipulate
Tear
Alter
Fix
Construct
Transform
Handle
Invent

A visual/spatial student likes to participate in activities that use these words.

Layout
Observe
Paint
Copy
Color
Scan
Pantomime
Inspect
Etch
Notice
Imagine
Chart
Look
Fantasize
Visual Activities
Sketch
See
Reproduce
Design
View
Mold
Illustrate

© 1994 Pieces of Learning

classify   think critically   categorize

see patterns

compare/contrast

predict solutions

create codes

The logical/mathematical student likes to participate in activities that use these words.

independent study

self-paced work

The intrapersonal student likes to participate in activities that use these words.

reflect on actions

journals   set goals   study cubicles

whistle and hum

appreciate different kinds of music

sing

play music

> The musical/rhythmic student likes to participate in activities that use these words.

play an instrument

group
brainstorming

board games

write music

music software

> The interpersonal student likes to participate in activities that use these words.

service learning

simulations

peer teaching

interactive software

people person

work in cooperative groups

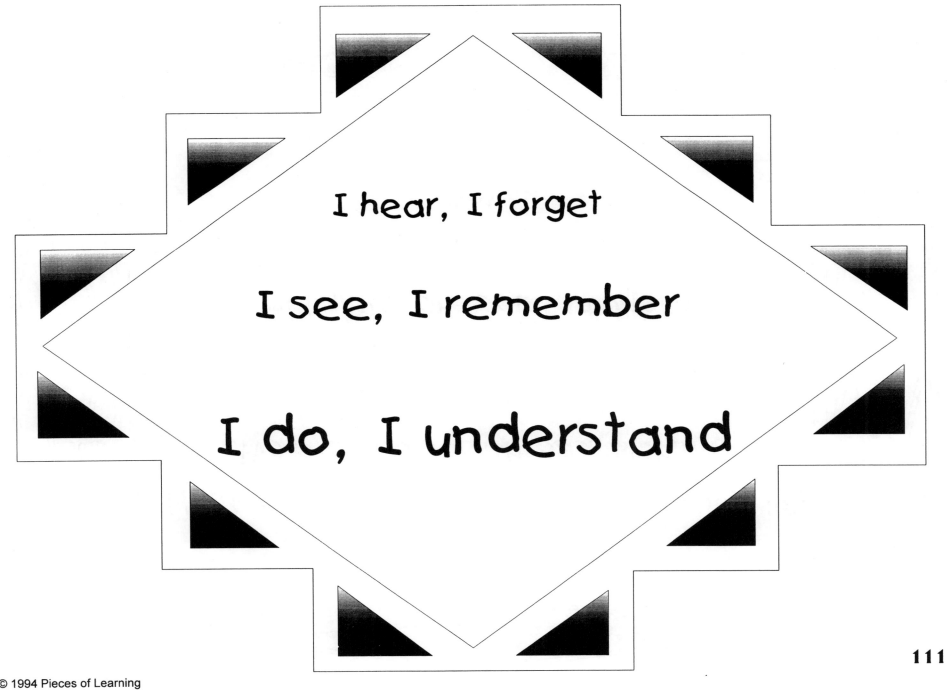

I hear, I forget

I see, I remember

I do, I understand

111

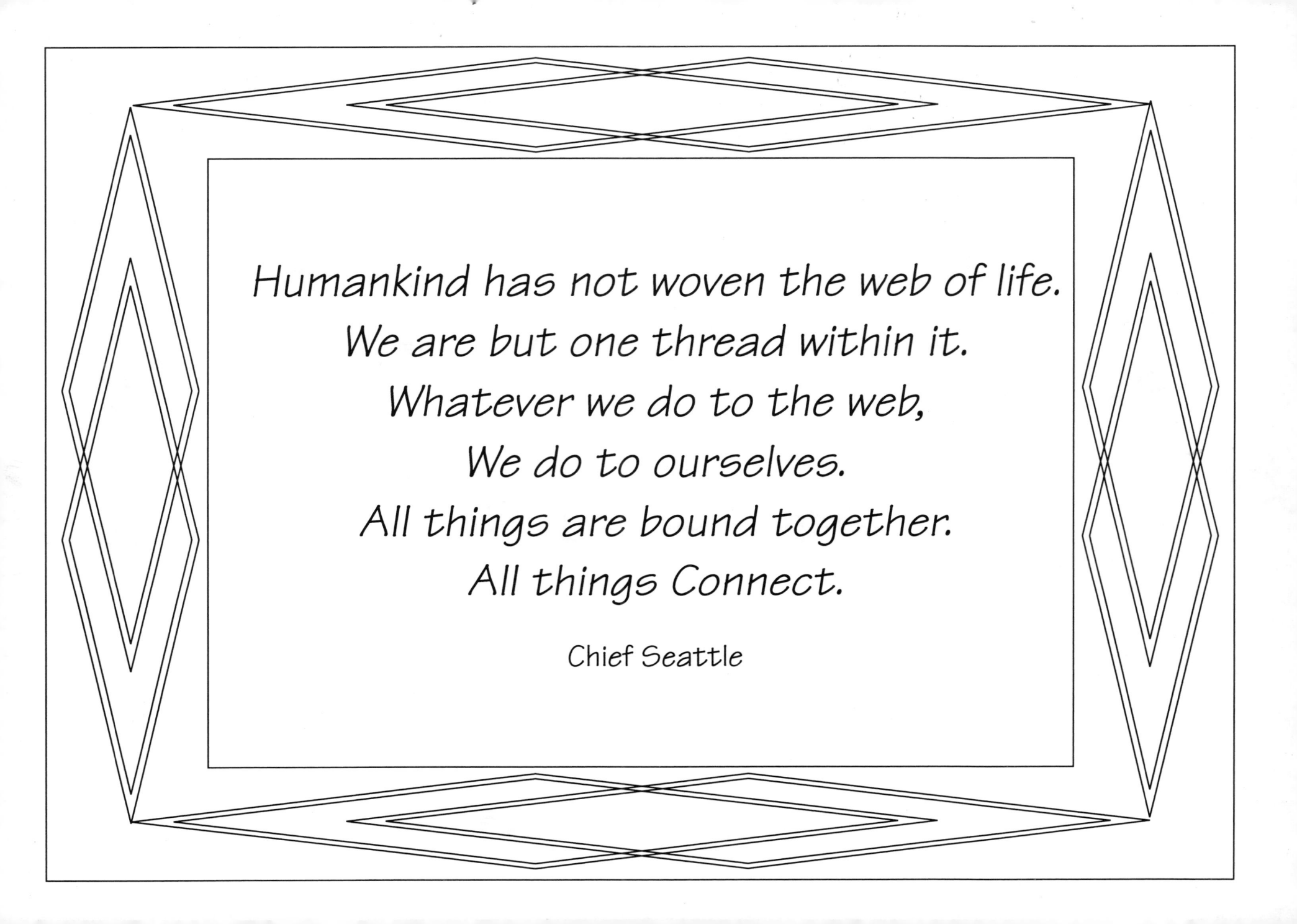

Humankind has not woven the web of life.
We are but one thread within it.
Whatever we do to the web,
We do to ourselves.
All things are bound together.
All things Connect.

Chief Seattle